Inclusion in the Primary Classroom

Practical resources to promote inclusion and disability awareness

www.teachingexpertise.com/teachtoinspire

Acknowledgements

I am indebted to:

- Nik and Ann from the 'Enable Me' team in Littlehampton for firing me up about inclusion of children with physical disabilities

- Milton Mount Primary School, West Sussex for allowing me to see the 'Enable Me' team in action and watch junior children designing an 'Enable Me' video

- Pupils of Connaught Junior school who drew and wrote for me and the 'Enable Me' team

- Year 2 pupils at Copythorne Infant School, Hampshire, for talking with me as well as drawing and writing for me

- George Robinson for his sensitive editing and good ideas

- Philippa Drakeford for her lovely drawings that make this book attractive.

Inclusion in the Primary Classroom

Practical resources to promote inclusion and disability awareness

Margaret Collins

Illustrated by

Philippa Drakeford

This book is created by Barbara Maines and George Robinson for Teach to Inspire, a series for Optimus Education.

Author

Margaret Collins

Designer

Jess Wright

Editors

George Robinson and Barbara Maines

Copy editor

Mel Maines

Illustrator

Philippa Drakeford

Printed by Hobbs the Printers Ltd.

Registered Office: Brunel Road, Totton, Hampshire SO40 3WX, UK

Registered Number: 422 132

Published by Optimus Education: a division of Optimus Professional Publishing Limited

Registered office: 33-41 Dallington Street, London EC1V 0BB

Registered number: 05791519

Telephone: 0845 450 6407 Fax: 0845 450 6410

www.teachingexpertise.com

ISBN 978-1-906517-06-9

A CD-ROM is attached to the inside front cover and is an integral part of this publication.

Contents

Use of the CD-ROM

Many Teach to Inspire publications include CD-ROMs to support the purchaser in the delivery of the training or teaching activities. These will include any of the following file formats:

- PDFs requiring Acrobat v.3
- Microsoft Word files
- Microsoft Powerpoint files
- Video clips which can be played by Windows Media Player
- If games are included the software required is provided on the CD.

All material on the accompanying CD-ROM can be printed by the purchaser/user of the book. This includes library copies. Some of this material is also printed in the book and can also be photocopied but this will restrict it to the black and white/greyscale version when there might be a colour edition on the CD-ROM.

The CD-ROM itself must not be reproduced or copied in its entirety for use by others without permission from the publisher.

Symbols key

 This symbol indicates a page that can be copied from the book or printed from the CD-ROM.

Introduction

Any discussion in schools about inclusion should address several important questions, for example, 'Do we value all children equally?', 'What do we mean by 'inclusion?', 'How do we get children to value inclusion and accept as equals those children who are not as able physically or mentally as they themselves are?'

Inclusion is about membership and belonging to a community. In schools it involves all kinds of practices that are ultimately practices of good teaching. Good teachers think thoughtfully about children and develop ways to reach every child in their care, regardless of their age, ability, gender, ethnicity, attainment or background. Such teachers will ensure that all children have an equal chance to realise their full potential.

Inclusive education means that all children in a school, no matter what their strengths or weaknesses in any area, become part of the school community. They are included and feel they belong in school among other children, teachers and support staff. As adults, people work in inclusive communities, with people of different abilities, disabilities, nationalities and religions; children of all ages should learn and grow in inclusive environments that mimic the places where they will eventually work.

More and more children with disabilities are entering mainstream education. In most cases their special needs will be catered for by extra help from support staff within or without the classroom. There has been an increase in the number of classroom assistants and special support assistants. Each school's Special Educational Needs Coordinator (SENCO) has the responsibility to coordinate the provision for children with special needs and liaise with fellow teachers. Their duty is also to manage learning support assistants (LSAs), liaise with external agencies, oversee the records of children with special educational needs as well as liaising with parents/carers. They organise statements and annual reviews.

However as well as this provision for including and educating children with special needs in our schools, we have also to think about the schools or classes where there may be no disabled or special needs children for other children to include. All children need education in considering the needs of children who are different in some way from themselves. They need to be personally involved in this and to have practice in thinking of ways to include children and others with special or specific needs. In considering how to include all children, they themselves will increase in self-esteem and become more emotionally literate. They will have a greater awareness of what is needed to improve society and make their world a better and fairer place for everyone.

> 'The millions of non-disabled students currently enrolled in schools are future firefighters, nurses, store clerks, teachers, job coaches, legislators, secretaries, physicians, school board members, employers, voters, doctors, lawyers, budget determiners, policy analysts, co-workers, police officers, and taxpayers. Approximately 15% of them will become parents of children with disabilities. A larger proportion will have a friend, neighbor, or relative who is the parent of a child with a disability and many others will be paid to provide services to people with disabilities.'
> **Lou Brown, University of Wisconsin, Madison.**

> 'When good inclusion is in place, the child who needs the inclusion does not stand out. The inclusive curriculum includes strong parental involvement, students making choices, and a lot of hands-on and heads-on involvement.'
> **Dr. Melissa Heston, Associate Professor of Education, University of Northern Iowa.**

The above quotes are from: http://www.uni.edu/coe/inclusion/philosophy/philosophy.html

Inclusion is not only about where children are educated; it's a philosophy that includes the whole school and it is everybody's responsibility. If we think back to the village school with one primary class, we find children aged from five to eleven years with one teacher. Children learned from one another, and the teacher was expected to teach all those in the class. Children with more normal development had a higher level of tolerance for, and acceptance of, children with any kind of difference.

Currently the Disability Discrimination Act (DDA) defines a disabled person as someone who has:

> 'a physical or mental impairment which has a substantial and long-term adverse effect on his or her ability to carry out normal day-to-day activities.'

The DDA also allows this basic definition to be modified for people who have mental impairments and progressive conditions, so that it sets out when people are to be treated as disabled. The DDA 2005 changes some of these things.

The DDA 2005 extends coverage of the DDA in the following ways:

- It removes the requirement in the DDA that a mental illness must be 'clinically well recognised' before it can count as an impairment for the purposes of the DDA. The Government has decided that this stipulation is no longer required. People with a mental illness will still need to show that their impairment has a long-term and substantial adverse effect on their ability to carry out normal day-to-day activities. By removing the 'clinically well-recognised' requirement, the Government has also brought DDA coverage for people with mental illnesses into line with coverage for all other mental and physical impairments.

- People with HIV, cancer and multiple sclerosis (MS) will be deemed to be covered by the DDA effectively from the point of diagnosis, rather than from the point when the condition has some adverse effect on their ability to carry out normal day-to-day activities. Extending the coverage of the DDA in this way will mean that the protection of the DDA will be afforded to another 250,000 disabled consumers.

See website: http://www.dwp.gov.uk/aboutus/provisions-dda.pdf

Disability Discrimination Act (DDA) 2001

The SEN and Disability Act 2001 amended the Disability Discrimination Act 1995. The Disability Discrimination Act (DDA) requires schools:

- not to treat disabled pupils 'less favourably'

- to make reasonable adjustments to ensure that disabled pupils are not at a substantial disadvantage

- to draw up plans to show how, over time, they will increase access to education for disabled pupils (school accessibility plans).

For more information see:
http://www.teachernet.gov.uk/wholeschool/sen/disabilityandthedda/

Promoting disability equality in schools

The Disability Discrimination Act 2001 sets out a general duty to promote disability equality with a specific duty which applies to local authorities and publicly-funded schools. This specific duty includes a requirement to prepare and publish a disability equality scheme showing how a public authority is meeting its general duty.

All primary schools must have a Disability Equality Scheme in place by December 2007.

Schools must demonstrate what they have done and what they plan to do to improve opportunities and outcomes for disabled pupils, staff, parents/carers and other users of the school. They must involve pupils, staff, parents/carers and others in the development of their scheme. Disabled people and those with special needs need to be involved from the very start and their involvement needs to inform the preparation, development, publication, review and reporting of the scheme.

Each school's disability equality scheme must show how the school takes a proactive approach to promoting disability equality, inclusion and eliminating discrimination. It must be explicit, comprehensive and involve disabled pupils, staff, parents/carers and other users of the school. It is illegal to treat a disabled pupil or prospective pupil less favourably than another for reasons related to their disability. Schools must ensure that every effort is made to cater for the disabled person's physical and mental needs. The governing body of the school is the 'responsible body' for the DDA duties and needs to ensure that everyone in the school, staff or volunteer, is aware of the duties owed to disabled pupils.

To avoid discrimination against any disabled pupil, all staff need to consider how they will implement the scheme in relation to their area of responsibility, for example,

- in the classroom; the class teacher
- on a school trip; the member of staff planning a school trip
- at dinner times and break times; the ancillary staff
- in a particular area of curriculum; those with curriculum responsibilities
- across the whole school; the head teacher.

The disability equality scheme should show how the school is accessible for disabled people and how teachers, ancillary staff and parents/carers have prepared for implementation of the scheme. Most schools now have disabled access, but it may be necessary to look at other areas of the building to decide if alterations need to be made or whether disabled children can be catered for in certain areas. These practical considerations are easy to define and implement.

However, there is more to disability equality than the written scheme, the practical considerations of the school building and the attitudes of the staff. Children have needs too, and not only those who are disabled. Both disabled and able-bodied children need help in recognising disabilities, both physical and mental and learning how to treat people with disabilities. We need to help children to understand:

- that there are different kinds of disabilities
- what they think it feels like to be disabled
- what they can do to help people who are disabled

- how they can show empathy towards disabled people
- how to interact with people and children who are disabled.

Through discussion, involvement and practical activities, able-bodied children can be made more aware of the needs and feelings of people who are disabled, have special needs or who are in some way different from them.

If we want non-disabled children to understand and feel empathy for those who are disabled or special, we need to try to put them in the shoes of a child or adult who is 'special'.

It seems to me that young children must be taught about disabilities, given language to use with, and learn how to react to, people who are in any way disabled. How are we going to do this? Asking disabled people to visit classrooms and talk to children is a valuable input, though not always possible. Through discussion, involvement and practical activities, able-bodied children can be made more aware of the needs and feelings of people who are disabled. The 'Enable Me' project in West Sussex seeks to do this.

The 'Enable Me' project

The 'Enable Me' team is an offshoot of the Shopmobility group in Littlehampton, Sussex (http://www.enableme.org.uk/). The team goes into schools to talk to children about disability and tries to help them to understand what being disabled means and how it doesn't necessarily need to stop people doing what they want. Many disabled people are spurred on to great things and see their disability as an incentive to overcome adversity. The team gives able-bodied children practice in using disability aids to try to help them to understand how people with various disabilities feel.

The Enable Me aims are:

- to improve and increase the children's knowledge about disabilities
- to help children to accept that all disabled people can contribute to society
- to create positive attitudes towards disability in future generations
- to challenge and change any of the children's perceived negative feelings about people with disabilities and to help them to relate to disabled people
- to increase the children's understanding of the difficulties that disabled people face through interactive use of disability aids.

The objectives are:

- through direct work with children in school, to raise awareness of disability issues in the wider community
- through practical activities with the children in school, to create a sense of excitement, fun and positivism around disability issues
- by using a role-model, to inspire children to overcome and challenge adversity in their own lives.

The Enable Me team visits schools in the West Sussex area to help children to understand the feelings of people with physical disabilities. Following a presentation given to the children, the team usually introduces someone with a disability who can talk about their life. Children are shown some disability aids and allowed to experiment with them and explore the feelings of people who have to use these. There is a general discussion about people with disabilities. Most schools follow up the work and give children the opportunity to write about the experience. Their comments often include surprise that the world can be an exciting and adventurous place for people with disabilities.

An example of the Enable Me team's work

In a school in Crawley, the Enable Me team is in action. After a brief presentation about the team's work, children are introduced to Swasie Turner, MBE, and hear him speak about his wonderful and uplifting fundraising activities following a devastating accident when he had been a police officer (see www.swasieturner.org). While this charismatic individual is an inspiration to those who are in wheelchairs, he is also helping able-bodied children and young people to know how to treat people with disabilities. Children who had seen a person in a wheelchair as someone to be pitied or ignored now see a different side to disability.

Swasie shows the children that even a disability such as his can be overcome; it can be an inspiration to do good things for the community; it can be seen as a challenge. Following this interaction there are practical activities for the children. They are, for example, able to use wheelchairs and find them difficult to manoeuvre! They use aids for the disabled and, through special glasses, view the world of the partially sighted. A discussion following these practical activities allows children to voice concerns and express appreciation of the work of the Enable Me team as well as admiration of Swasie's work.

Researching children's perceptions of disability

As part of a tool to evaluate the success of the Enable Me team's work, children were asked to write what advice they might give to someone who was disabled and would not be able to walk again. In collection of base line data, which took place before any input from the team, one Year 6 girl wrote:

> 'nouthing, because can't speek to people that hve something rong with them because it makes me upser.' [sic]

This seems to be a universal worry for children – they may have been told not to stare at, or to look away from, people who are disabled. If the girl had already been involved in work to raise awareness, hopefully this kind of statement would not have been made.

A small research task

I worked with a Year 2 class talking with the children about people who are able-bodied and those who are not. I introduced the words 'disability' and 'disabled' and explained that these were the acceptable words to use to, and about, people who are not able-bodied. I explained that some disabled people had temporary disabilities that would get better and that some had permanent disabilities that would never get better. After discussing this I explained that some people had disabilities that you could see and others were disabled in a way that you wouldn't notice. After discussion, I asked the children if they knew people who were disabled in each of these ways and they told me about people they knew. I asked them to do some drawing and writing for me so that we could talk about their own opinions later.

I asked them to:

- draw someone with a disability that shows; to write what the disability is and how they think the person feels about being disabled
- draw someone with a disability that doesn't show; to write what that disability is and how they think that that person feels.

Because a boy in the class had just returned to school with a broken leg, many of the disabilities you could see were of this type. We discussed the kinds of disabilities that you can see and the long list of feelings they had written, all feelings of sadness, loneliness or unhappiness.

We talked then about disabilities that you can't see. Some had written that they couldn't see what the disability was, others mentioned brain damage and people who are blind and deaf. We agreed that these disabilities were difficult to understand because the people looked just like everyone else.

One child wrote, 'doesn't kn wote ansthi is because her bran isnt woknue propley,' (doesn't know what anything is because her brain isn't working properly).

Another wrote, 'sad but happy at same time because of friends.'

This was a wonderful way in to talk about the importance of friends to people who are disabled. We talked about what disabled people could do and couldn't do and how they might feel about their disabilities. I asked them if they thought that people in a wheelchair could lead a normal life and they mostly shook their heads.

The children were shown a photograph downloaded from Swasie Turner's website and told about some of the things he had done. They were then questioned again and this time more positive responses were given as many children recognised that viewing disability as a challenge is a way of overcoming it.

They were also shown a photograph of Alex McGlory who has cerebral palsy. In the photograph he is sitting in his wheelchair coaching able-bodied children also in wheelchairs in the art of playing wheelchair basketball. Alex had spoken to me of his work with able-bodied children in Littlehampton and said that he didn't mind people asking him about his disability if they asked in a polite way – not rudely or unkindly. He said, 'Think of my feelings, think of everyone's feelings. Try to be helpful, for example, ask if the person would like help in a kind say, saying, for example, 'Do you need the door opening?" He also said, 'But don't assume that people can't do things. My chair helps me to do things, so does my car and my crutch.' He went on to say that he thought it important for children to know that all people are different; some are nice and some are horrible; disabled people are just the same – some nice, some not so nice.

These Year 2 children were asked how they could help disabled children, comments included:

- I would give them some money.
- I'd tell them about wheelchair basketball.
- I would say to him, 'Are you alright? Would you like me to do anything while I'm here?'
- 'If you're feeling very sad, I will get you some dinner or something. I'll do you some housework or go to the shop.'
- I'd say, 'Are you OK?'

The children were asked what they had to think about when they see disabled people in the shops or in the town. Responses included, 'saying things in a kind way', 'bending down to talk to them if they were in a wheelchair' and 'thinking about how they would feel'.

Children who are disabled

Some disabled people, especially children, find it hard to let people know how they themselves feel. Perhaps on admitting such a child to school we should find out the child's own feelings about the life they have to lead. Though it is not easy for young children to find the words to say what they mean, we can tap into their feelings with the following short Draw and Write activity in Unit 1. Their responses could be very helpful to others in knowing how this particular child feels and how he likes to be treated. The response sheet could alert adults in school to understand the child's needs, be done annually and attitudes noted in the child's records.

Disability equality is really important and implementation of the DDA will go a long way towards full inclusion; but this book is not only about those who are disabled. Other children have special needs too, sometimes only short term. We have a duty to educate all children to understand the feelings of disabled people or those with special needs and to know how to include them. Able-bodied children need to know that though disabled people may (or may not) look different on the outside, they usually feel just the same as we do on the inside.

There should be a school-wide policy in using the correct language. 'Disability' is the word to use; children need to know that this is acceptable and not use 'cripple' or other often used unkind words; certainly not 'handicapped' because disabled people are not handicapped. We need to help the disabled to feel 'enabled' to do all the things of which they are capable.

Extra provision that you may need to consider

All schools are different and so according to the children they are educating they will have varying needs. Your school may need:

- well trained learning support assistants able to work with children with special needs
- learning support assistants to work with pupils with English as an additional language
- translators for non English speaking children on entry to school
- support assistants to work with children who are in wheelchairs
- specifically trained people to work with children who have hearing loss, are partially sighted, or who have other specific health conditions
- a member of staff responsible for supporting inclusion
- adults competent to run anger management courses for pupils
- a pupil support service, available for children who feel they have problems
- peer support groups to help children with special needs and others
- a trained person to provide individual counselling for pupils where necessary
- to consider implementing mediation or peer massage as an aid to calming children
- support groups for parents/carers of children with disabilities or special needs.

The work and activities you will find in this book demand commitment, belief and time but will ensure that disabled and disadvantaged children feel included and that all children have both empathy and skills to ensure that inclusion happens.

When asked to write what she would say to someone newly disabled who had to use a wheelchair, a Year 6 girl wrote,

> 'I would say don't worry, you're exactly the same as anyone else, but in a wheelchair.'

What you get in this book

This book is designed as a programme for mainstream primary school children. It will also be of use to teachers or special needs assistants working with children with special needs, teachers in special schools, hospice schools, hospital teachers, teacher or nursery training establishments and youth groups.

It is not necessary to use the sections in any particular order. Teachers who encounter specific problems or children with certain conditions may find it useful to tap into relevant sections.

It will be a useful addition to PSHE curriculum materials.

This book is intended to alert teachers and others to any problems with regard to children including, or not including, others in their schools or settings. It is not only about disability or disabled children. It has several specific sections, each containing activities with the emphasis on inclusion.

Privileged people

This is a Circle Time activity that is designed to help children to experience privilege and exclusion.

The sections and units

There are two sections with a total of eight units.

The first section, Units 1 and 2, is about people with disabilities.

The second section, Units 3 to 8, is about people who are not disabled but who have other conditions.

Section 1. People with disabilities

Unit 1. The disabled child's point of view

It is important for young disabled children to have a voice. It can be difficult for any young children to voice their concerns or problems as many will have limited use of language and small vocabulary. By giving them the chance to draw a picture of their point of view and then to talk or write about their picture we may be able to gain some insight into how they see themselves in relation to the rest of the children they will be learning with and to understand any concerns, strengths and weaknesses.

There are two activities in this unit.

This first activity is a simple draw and write or draw and talk exercise for children arriving at school with a specific disability or medical condition. It is assumed that the child will complete this on arriving at school. Their responses will make their feelings known to the adults in school. This could be repeated at the beginning of each year to monitor change and to help the teacher of the new class to understand the child's feelings.

The second activity is for older children already at school, moving in from another school or who contract a disability while at your school. It too will provide a platform for the child's voice to be heard. Again, it is suggested that this could be repeated annually. There are two copiable response sheets.

Unit 2. Children with disabilities or medical conditions

This unit is concerned with how we act towards children and others who are different in some physical or medical way. It is not only concerned with the feelings of the disabled child but with the feelings and actions of the rest of the children in the class.

Section 2. People with other conditions

Unit 3. Groups we belong to

This is about the groups to which children belong and how to include others in these various groups so that no one will feel rejected.

Unit 4. Nationality, religion and socio-economic difference

This is about including children from various nationalities, religions and socio-economic groups; how we act towards children and adults who have a different background or culture to the one we have.

Unit 5. Speech and language differences

This is about how we understand, accept and act towards children who speak differently from most children in the school; this includes children with speech impairment, accents and language problems.

Unit 6. Gender roles and stereotypes

This is about how adults and children act towards those of the opposite gender with activities concerned with gender expectations and stereotyping.

Unit 7. Bullying and low self-esteem

This is about bullying, name calling, threatening behaviour and low self-esteem.

Unit 8. Children with other special educational needs

This is about children with other special educational needs: learning difficulties, behaviour difficulties, personality differences.

Appendix

Resources, books, websites and posters.

There are nine colour A3 posters for the eight units and the Privilidged People activity that can be found on the accompanying CD-Rom and A4 black and white versions in the appendix.

Structure of the lessons

Each unit starts with an introduction page. This explains the content of the unit and lists the various activities for the children. Where relevant there are also details of websites that could be useful for teachers or children.

The paired sets of activities on each double page provide activities more suitable for younger children on the left hand page and those for older children on the right, enabling teachers to 'mix and pick', selecting activities appropriate for the children in their care. Some activities take place in Circle Time, others rely on short stories or scenarios to set the scene for discussion and prepare the children for later activities. There are a few suggestions for work to be done at home.

The Circle Time activities are mainly for younger children although this format could be used for older children. There are no instructions for organising Circle Time in this book. It is felt that there are sufficient other resources for this and many schools now hold a regular Circle Time as part of their classroom organisation. Those not familiar with the organisation and running of Circle Time will find suitable resources in the appendix.

There are several paired copiable activity sheets for each unit, one of each pair for younger children and one for older children, both on the same theme. Teachers in some classes may like to use both activity sheets with children in their class in order to cater for various abilities. These could be taken home to encourage parent/carer participation.

At the end of each unit there are extension activities, again in pairs for younger and older children including a research activity to encourage children to find out more.

A reflect and remember page concludes each unit.

Just a start!

It is hoped that teachers will use the activities as a starting point for further work on each theme. According to the needs and abilities of the children and the situation in which they find themselves, children themselves may be encouraged to find out more about each unit.

Are you an includer?

You may feel this is an appropriate question to ask your children to help them to focus on helping children to include others. You could use this as a slogan while doing this work. There are a few references to this in the activities.

Sensitivity warning

You will need to be sensitive to children in your class who have special needs and you may like to amend some of the activities where these might upset or point to certain children. You will be reminded about the sensitivity issue on some activities with a note 'Sensitivity warning'.

Note: To avoid the tiresome repetitive use of 'he or she', 'him or her', the masculine has been used throughout this book. This in no way suggests any gender bias.

Privileged people – a Circle Time activity

The following is a Circle Time activity to help children experience the feelings of exclusion, discrimination or lack of privilege.

Use this activity before you start the activities in this book. It is designed to help children to experience what it feels like if they are discriminated against. You can adapt it in the light of your current practice of rewards. In essence, the 'game' is to give one group something to do that they won't like very much and to give the other group rewards.

Immediately after the activity you will need to explain to the children what you have been doing and ask how each group felt when they were doing their part of the game. It would be enjoyable for the children if you change the groups and repeat the game.

Privileged people

In Circle Time give each alternate child a number one or two.

Ask all the ones to walk around the circle once backwards until they get to their place.
Ask all the twos to give you a big smile.

Ask all the ones to jump up and down five times and then sit down again.
Ask all the twos to sit and have a rest.

Ask all the ones to sit still and close their eyes without speaking for one minute.
Ask all the twos to go and get a piece of fruit.

Ask all the ones to walk heel to toe across the circle and change places with another one.
Ask all the twos to go and get a smiley sticker.

Ask the ones to tell you how they feel. Ask the twos to tell you how they feel.
Do the children think that you have been fair to them all?

Explain to the children that during this Circle Time you have been deliberately trying to help them to experience how it feels to be discriminated against or excluded.

Reverse the process and ask the children how they feel now. Remind them that the feelings they experienced when they weren't the favoured group are the feelings that other children will experience if they are excluded from work, groups or games.

Section 1
People with disabilities

Unit 1. The disabled child's point of view

Unit 2. Children with disabilities or medical conditions

Resources for this section on the CD-ROM:

Coloured posters for Unit 1 and Unit 2 and the paired activity sheets.

1

Unit 1. The disabled child's point of view

A one-off activity on initial entry of the child to school. Format one.

When children with some kind of disability first arrive in school, the pre-school adults, parents/carers and teachers will have discussed the condition and how this will impinge on the child's school life. There may be little insight into how the child himself feels, perhaps because it can be difficult to intrude on the child's feelings in case he is made to feel even more different or because he lacks confidence and finds it difficult to talk about feelings to strangers. It is much less threatening to ask a child to draw a picture and to either talk or write about it. This also has the advantage of providing a reference point for later in the child's education.

> This unit provides an opportunity for disabled children either at entry to school or who are already at school to express their views and feelings about their situation.

It is suggested that the child's response sheet is kept as a record, together with notes made by the teacher during and after the session. In this way there will be a record of the child's feelings about the disability and about his feelings towards coming to school.

Draw and Talk for Year 1

After the first term or year in school you could use format two and keep these response sheets with the original drawn responses.

Draw and Write for following years

As the child matures and is able to write, you could use format three.

Immediately following each activity

When the child has finished the activity you will naturally praise him for his work. Use this opportunity to talk about what he has drawn, talked about or written. You will probably need to clarify some of his responses and reassure him about any concerns. Make a brief note of these concerns on the child's actual response sheet. You may wish to write up fuller notes to accompany this as a record of how the child really feels.

It could be very useful to share these response sheets and any of the child's concerns with the parents or carers and discuss any implications of what the child has drawn and said.

On initial entry to school, at age four. Format one.

If possible this drawing activity should take place before the child starts school. Perhaps the Year R teacher could be given a little time to spend with the child on an initial visit to school or during a home visit. After putting the child at ease, perhaps by sharing a picture book if at home, or showing him around the classroom if at school, the teacher could take the child to a quiet place, such as the library and ask him to draw himself coming to

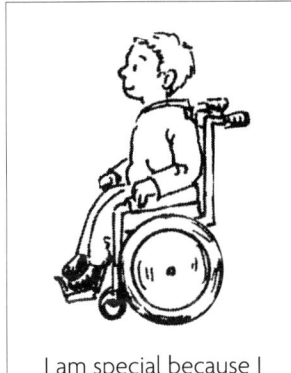

I am special because I have a wheelchair.

the school and then to talk or write about how he thinks he will feel. To keep this a positive exercise the child could be encouraged to see himself as special in some positive way – the specialness being because of his disability or medical condition.

Activity instructions

Give the child a piece of A4 paper and ask him to draw himself. As he is drawing ask him to talk about the drawing and why he is special. When the drawing is finished ask him to finish your sentence, 'I am special because...'

On the other side of the paper ask the child to draw anything that he thinks will help him to do well at school. What we want to know is how he feels about coping with school, so the emphasis will be on feelings. After he has drawn his picture, ask him to tell you about the things he has drawn and ask him if you can label them. Ask him to tell you how he feels about coming to school and ask if you can write this for him on his paper.

Praise him for his pictures and for what he has told you. Talk about what he has said and reassure him about any concerns. Say that you want to keep this picture to remind you of what he has said. If he wants to take it home to show his family make a photocopy for him and keep the original as your record.

For children already at school or older children moving to your school

As we really want to know how the child feels about being at school with this condition or disability, specific questions are asked about this and the child invited to respond. It is suggested that you repeat this exercise at the start of each school year and keep the response sheets as a record of how the child's feelings and needs change.

The activity asking children to draw then talk about their drawing or to draw then write about their drawings has four parts. Rather than use the words 'condition or disability' in the following script, it would be better to substitute the exact word or phrase, for example, 'your eczema', or 'being in your wheelchair'.

The Draw and Talk activity for younger children. Format two.

1. Draw yourself in your classroom coping with... (your condition or disability).

   Tell me what you are doing and how you are feeling.

2. Draw yourself with a group of friends in the playground.

   Tell me what you are doing and how you are feeling.

3. Draw a grown-up at school that you can talk to about... (your condition or disability).

   Tell me this person's name and what you are saying to them.

4. Draw yourself feeling good at school with... (your condition or disability).

   Tell me some of the good things about how your school can help you to cope.

Tell me what else you think your school could do to support you and make you feel better about being here and I will write this on the back of your paper.

Draw and Write for older children. Format three.

1. Draw yourself in your classroom coping with... (your condition or disability).

   Write what you are doing and how you are feeling.

2. Draw yourself with a group of friends in the playground.

   Write what you are doing and how you are feeling.

3. Draw a grown-up at school who you can talk to about... (your condition or disability).

   Write the person's name and what you are saying to them.

4. Draw yourself feeling good at school with... (your condition or disability).

   Write down some of the good things about how your school can help you to cope.

What else could your school do to support you and make you feel better about being here? Write this on the back of your paper.

Suggested activity sheet outlines are on the following pages. The Draw and Talk Response Sheet has space for the drawing at the top and a box for the teacher to write below.

Draw and Talk Response Sheet

1.	2.
3.	4.

Draw and Write Response Sheet

1. Draw here.	2. Draw here.
Write here.	Write here.
3. Draw here.	4. Draw here.
Write here.	Write here.

Unit 2. Children with disabilities or medical conditions

We really want all children to understand and feel empathy for children with disabilities or medical conditions. This unit is not only concerned with the feelings of the disabled child but with the feelings and actions of the rest of the children in the class.

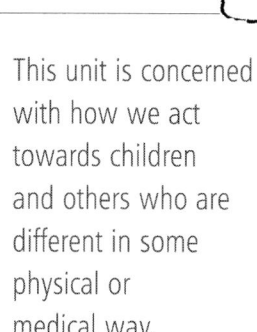

This unit is concerned with how we act towards children and others who are different in some physical or medical way.

You may well not have any disabled children in either your class or school but it is important to give the children the understanding both of how these children may feel and how they themselves should react to them.

In this unit after considering how we are all the same and different in part 1, we will be considering children who have a specific medical condition under the following headings:

- Same and different
- New to the school
- Those with hearing difficulties
- Those partially sighted or blind
- Temporary and permanent health conditions
- Eczema and other skin conditions
- Those who need a wheelchair.

There are paired activity sheets at the end of the unit.

Useful websites

Teachers might find the British Sign Language (BSL) website useful for children to visit; it gives signs and video clips.

http://www.britishsignlanguage.com/

http://www.bbc.co.uk/health/conditions/

http://lenmac.tripod.com/celebrities.html

Same and different – younger children

Circle Time

In Circle Time talk about how we are all the same and yet all very different in so many ways. Ask the children to tell you how they are the same, for example, two eyes, hair, faces. Then ask the children to say how they are all different, for example, blue eyes, tall, long hair.

Remind the children about being kind in making comments about other children. Ask them to think of two or three permanent attributes for a child they know and ask each of them to finish the sentence:

'My friend ... (name) always has ... (for example, brown eyes and fair hair).'

Now ask them to think of things that change, for example, clothes, hair styles and to do the same activity naming these when finishing the following sentence:

'My friend ... (name) sometimes has black shoes and hair in a ponytail.'

Drawing activity

Ask the children to draw a picture of themselves and to use one colour to write a label for each of the things that are always the same. Ask them to use a different colour to write labels for things that can change.

On the other side of the paper ask them to draw someone who is different from them and to write how this person is different.

Group activity

Use the children's pictures as a resource and discuss the pictures they have drawn about children who are different. Talk specifically about whether they have drawn:

- only people with differences in appearance
- only people with physical differences
- any children with mental disabilities
- anyone with a medical condition.

Remind the children that though in your class they may be nearly all the same as each other, there are other children with physical and mental differences. Ask them to talk to their families about people like this and bring some ideas to Circle Time next time.

Same and different — older children

Circle Time

Discuss with the children the fact that we are all the same, but have slight differences. Ask them to consider how they are different from a friend of the same gender and how they are different from a friend of the opposite gender.

Ask for contributions that answer the questions, 'Are we the same?' and 'Are we different?'

Discuss how we feel when we are with people who are like us and how we feel when we are with people that we are not like.

Being sensitive to their qualities, ask if any can finish the sentence, 'I am different because...' Ask these children to say how they feel about the way they are different from other people. If they say they feel bad, discuss what you could all do to make things better.

Talk about the clothes we wear. Do the children like wearing their school uniform so that they look the same? Do they wear the same kind of clothes as their friends when they are out of school? Do they like to wear things that are way out or different? Do they prefer to wear the same style of clothes? Discuss their reasons for these likes and dislikes.

Discuss stereotyping, such as the 'dumb blonde' type or the 'strong silent type'. Do they think that all people who look a certain way have similar characteristics?

Data line

Discuss the kinds of things that make us feel good and not so good about ourselves. Is it better to project a positive image even when we feel low or is it OK to look down and despondent? Ask the children to make a data line to show what they think; one end of the line to represent 'always look positive however you feel' and the other end of the line to represent 'always show your true feelings'. Children can place themselves in-between these two extremes. Ask volunteers to justify why they chose to place themselves there. Discuss the implications about how other people would view us.

Research activity

Ask or help the children to think up a grid or format for collecting data about the feelings of six or more people at home. Ask them to find out whether these six or more people feel:

- good about all their personal qualities
- good about some of their qualities
- bad about most of their qualities.

Ask them to write down what they think would make each person feel better.

2

New to the school – younger children

Tell a story

Jonah lived in a country village and went to the small village school. When his parents decided to move to the town, they took him to look at the school nearest to their new home. It was a very big school. It had lots of children. The playground was huge and at playtime it looked busy and dangerous. When Jonah got home and his dad asked him about his new school, Jonah burst into tears and said, 'I don't want to go to that school.'

Jonah felt...

sad, unhappy, miserable, worried, anxious, scared, fed up, lonely.

Ask the children to think of all the feelings Jonah might have had about the new school. Make a list of these feelings and talk about where in Jonah's body he might have felt these feelings.

Ask the children if they have ever felt like this. Can they remember where in their bodies they felt bad?

Draw a picture

Ask the children to draw a picture of Jonah talking to his dad after visiting the school. Ask them to write in speech bubbles what they think Jonah said to his dad and what his dad said. Talk about what the children wrote and whether what Dad said would help Jonah. What do they think would have been the best thing for Dad to say?

What could the teacher do?

Ask the children to think about Jonah coming to their school. He feels unhappy and lonely but the teacher is kind. What do you think the teacher would do or say? Ask the children to finish the sentence, 'I think the teacher would...'

What could you do in the classroom?

Now think of the children in the classroom. What kinds of things could the children say and do to make Jonah feel included in their class. Make a list of these under the heading 'Let's include Jonah in our classroom'.

What could you do in the playground?

Think about playtimes at your school; think about Jonah feeling lost and lonely there. What could you do to help him to feel included? Are you a good includer?

New to the school – older children

Discussion

Discuss with the children all the feelings that they could have when they go to a new place for the first time. Make a list of these. Explain that a child new to their school or classroom could feel all these feelings and probably more. Help the children to realise that going into a closed circle of people who all know each other can be really daunting and that their role in this situation is to help the person to feel included. Explain to the children that they have a very positive role to play in making sure that children are included, both in their classroom and in the playground.

How would you feel?

Set a scenario where the children in your class are individually going to another school where they know no one and do not know the rules. Ask them to help you to make a list of all the things that they would find difficult and write this up somewhere for everyone to see. It will include, for example, rules about meals, organisation or playtimes, assembly rituals, library rules, coming into the school, playground, classroom as well as extra class clubs or outings. Ask them to work individually to list the things that they think would worry them the most. From their list ask them to choose the four most worrying and to write a sentence or two about each one. Discuss these in Circle Time or discussion time.

Who could help?

Explore with the children the same scenario with lots of people who want to help. Who would these people be? How could they help? What could they do? Ask the children to work in small groups and to write a list of people who will help and beside their name, the things that they could do to help. Ask them to answer the question, 'Are you a good includer?'

Write a story

Ask the children to write a four part story about a new child coming into their class.

1. Write about the child's feelings, the child's parents' or grown-ups' feelings before they come to school.

2. The preparation that the teacher does to ensure inclusion.

3. The child's first day with details about who helps to include them.

4. What the child says and does when he gets home.

Display the stories. Discuss with the children which stories have the best ideas of how to integrate a newcomer into your class.

Can they write a list of 'Do's and Don'ts' to display?

Those with hearing difficulties – younger children

Remind the children that we are all different but that some children have greater differences than others.

Circle Time

Talk about our senses and especially about hearing. Ask the children to cover their ears and to look carefully at your face. Using no sound, talk to them for a minute about something interesting, such as holidays or a school event. Ask them to uncover their ears and to raise a thumb if they know what you were talking about.

Ask volunteers to finish the sentence, 'I think you were talking about...'

Talk about the problems that people with limited hearing have and ask the children to think about being someone who has a hearing difficulty. Can they imagine what it would feel like? Can anyone tell the group?

What could grown-ups and the school do?

Ask the children for their ideas about how adults and the school could help children with a hearing loss. Do they know that sometimes people can wear special hearing aids? Do they know that there are people who have the skill of sign language? Do they know that people with no hearing may speak in a different way because they have never heard words spoken?

What could you do?

Talk about the things that we can do to help people with poor hearing, for example, to speak clearly and slowly and to make sure the person can see your mouth. They can make sure that the child with restricted hearing is not left out of groups and group games because of their hearing loss. Just because someone can't hear doesn't mean that they are not clever and capable in all other ways. They can make sure that they don't treat the child as if they are not the same as everyone else, just because they can't hear.

Signs

Ask the children to work in pairs to write a list of signs or objects that we could use to help people who can't hear, for example, a light that flashes when the school bell goes. Ask them then to devise and draw some signs or objects that they could use in your classroom with a person who can't hear; they could draw them and write alongside each what it means.

Ask children to visit the British Sign Language website and learn some of their signs.

Those with hearing difficulties — older children

Explain to the children that there are various degrees of hearing loss. Some people have difficulty hearing for a short time, perhaps after an illness. This kind of hearing loss will get better. Some people can hear just a few of the sounds we have in our words but have difficulty when they can't see the speaker's face. Some people can be helped by having hearing aids; some can have implants to help them to hear a little. Others who are profoundly deaf may need to use sign-language or to lip read. Remind the children that children with poor hearing normally have all their other senses intact. Because they can't hear well doesn't mean that they can't think and reason. It is really important to make sure that we include children with a disability such as this into the whole of the school day. Exclusion isn't an option.

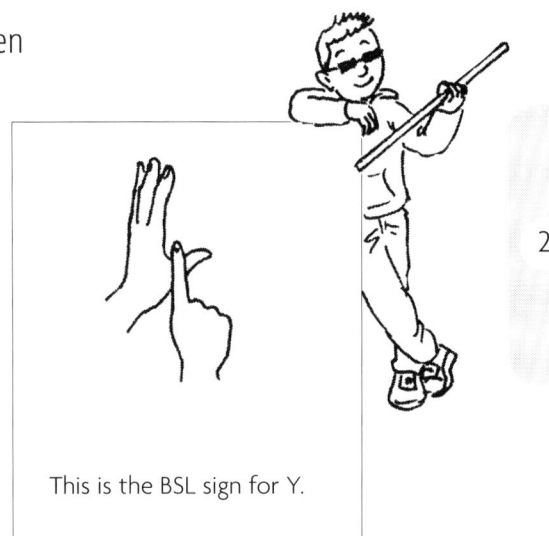

This is the BSL sign for Y.

How would it feel?

Ask the children to work in pairs with one trying to communicate a sentence with signs and lips. Can their partner understand? Ask them to change over and use a different sentence.

Use the TV or video and ask children to watch for a few minutes with the sound turned off. Can the children understand everything that is going on or do they just get a rough idea? How do they feel about this? Are they frustrated or angry because they can't understand everything? Remind them that this is how children with limited hearing may feel.

What can I do?

Working in small groups, ask the children to imagine that their best friend was suddenly unable to hear anything. Ask them to make a list of all the things they could do to make sure that they include this friend in every part of school life. Make sure they remember the playground and dinner room. Ask them to think about making sure that this friend can understand jokes and funny stories.

Find out at home

Ask the children to find out about people who have a hearing difficulty. If they put 'deaf' into an internet search engine they will find out a lot. They will see the American Sign Language (ASL) at: http://www.lifeprint.com/

Ask them to compare ASL to BSL, using the websites: http://www.britishsignlanguage.com/

Can they draw ASL or BSL signs for their first name?

Do they think there will be confusion and arguments in the limited hearing world about which to use?

Those partially sighted or blind — younger children

Circle Time

Tell the children you are all going to close your eyes for one minute. Use a timer. At the end of the minute ask the children to say what it felt like not to be able to see. What sounds did they hear? Did they learn anything? Do the same exercise with partially closed eyes. Ask volunteers to say how they felt when totally blind and partially sighted. List these words and try to put them in some kind of order.

scary, uncomfortable, worrying, nothing, can't do anything.

How do they feel?

Think about how someone without perfect sight would feel if they came to your school. Some children can wear spectacles; these can have very thick lenses and may look different from the usual spectacles. They may not help them to see as well as people with normal vision. Some children may not be able to see at all. Talk about how such children might feel.

What can you do?

People who cannot see often develop a really good sense of touch. They may want to touch your face so that they can feel what you look like. You can help by remembering that it is only their sight that is affected and that in every other way they are just like you. They will ask for help if they need it. You may like to ask them if they need help. If someone with partial sight comes to your class you can help a lot by including them in your groups and in games, giving them a role that they can play easily.

Tell a story

When Alice was born she could not see. There was no operation to help her and so she would have to live her life without sight. She went to a special school where all the children were partially sighted or totally blind. She learned to read, using Braille; she walked with a cane. Alice quickly learned to read Braille and loved reading. She had a special overlay on the computer so she could write and print off what she had written. Alice was really happy at school and had lots of friends. She also had a guide dog, Duke, to help her to get about. She loved Duke; he was her best friend.

Invite someone who is partially sighted to come and talk to the children. If they have a guide dog helper, ask them to talk about the dog, its needs and how it helps.

Those partially sighted or blind – older children

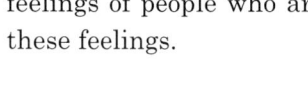

Circle Time

Discuss the kinds of problems that face children who are blind or partially sighted. Talk about the aids they can use to help them to get about and to live a normal life. Ask the children to think of how a person who is blind from birth would feel about going to school and the things they have to learn. Ask them to think about the problems a person who has an accident and becomes blind would have to face and how they would feel.

Ask the children to close their eyes and try to think of the feelings of people who are not able to see. Make a list of these feelings.

> The real problem of blindness is not the loss of eyesight. The real problem is the misunderstanding and lack of information that exists. If a blind person has proper training and opportunity, blindness can be reduced to a physical nuisance.
>
> (NFB website)

Drama experience

In a drama session, ask the children to work in pairs, one unable to see, perhaps using a blindfold; the other child as the helper. Give each pair tasks to do, for example, find a chair and sit in it, walk over to the window and pretend to close the curtains. Make sure they change roles. After the session, initiate a general discussion about the problems facing people who have partial sight or who are blind.

What can you do?

Read the above quotation from the National Federation for the Blind website to the children. Ask them to think of how they should relate to people who are blind or partially sighted. Ask the children to think how blind and partially sighted people would like to be treated. What kind of help would they like, or not like? How could they be included in normal life at home and out in the wider world? What kind of things could help them to live a normal life?

Be positive

Ask the children to work in pairs to make a list of things that a blind person can do.

Find out at home

Ask them to use books and the internet to find out about people who cannot see well, people such as Helen Keller who overcame blindness. Use websites such as Royal National Institute for the Blind (RNIB) or National Federation for the Blind (NFB). List the aids that are available for people who are blind or partially sighted.

Temporary and permanent health conditions — younger children

Circle Time

Talk to the children about being ill and being well. Explain that most of us have an illness from time to time and that most of these illnesses will get better with the right treatment. There are some other illnesses or health conditions that may not get better or that may need special drugs or treatment to control them. Ask the children to name some of the illnesses they know. Make a two part list and add to it by talking about all the people you know of who have health differences.

These will get better:
measles, flu, bad cold, cough.

These might need to be controlled:
MS, Spina Bifida, Diabetes, Downs Syndrome, Epilepsy.

Some will need help

If you have, or have had, children in your school with particular health conditions talk about these with the children. Explain that sometimes children may need a helper so that they can get about at school, or they may need someone to explain things to them or help them with reading and writing. Talk about how children feel when they are different and need special help. Will they be happy or sad about being 'different'?

Tell a story

> Anwar has diabetes. This means that he has a condition that has to be cared for most carefully. He has to have injections of insulin every day but now he is six he can do these himself while his mother watches. Anwar has to be careful that he doesn't get overtired or excited or this could make his blood sugar levels wrong. He has a special friend Dan at school who always keeps a watch out for him. Dan will tell the teacher or mid-day supervisor if he thinks Anwar needs help. Anwar is really glad to have this special friend so that he can live a normal life at school.

What could you do?

Think about health conditions that children might have at your school and how you could help. Will you treat children who are different in some way as normal and healthy? Will you include them in your games? Will you befriend them in the classroom and playground? Will you keep an eye out in case they need help? If so you are a good includer!

Health Activity Sheet 1

Ask the children to complete this and use it for discussion.

Temporary and permanent health conditions – older children

Discuss with the children the various health problems they have had from time to time, such as colds, chicken pox. Make a list of these on the board and ask who has had each illness, putting the number of children alongside the illness. Now talk about permanent health conditions and make a list of all the ones that the children can tell you. Explain that many conditions are controlled by drugs and medicines and that in this way, and with some help, children can live a normal life in and out of school. Discuss the implications of children with such conditions coming to school and how they can be helped to fit in and be included in the every day life of the school.

Online research

Ask pairs of children to visit the website: http://www.bbc.co.uk/health/conditions/ and to choose one of the health conditions there. Ask them to write a brief description of the condition, how it is controlled and how children with this condition can attend normal school. List any restrictions and any help the child might need. Share this research and create a three column chart with headings: 'health condition', 'particular needs of the child' and 'ways in which children with these can be integrated into school life'.

What can you do?

Talk about any children in your school with a health condition and help the children to understand their needs. Help them to understand that the most important need is for the child to be accepted and included in all class and play activities. Talk about being a good includer. It's not just a case of allowing children to join groups; children with health conditions need to feel really accepted and wanted and valued for what they can bring to the activity, the group and the school. Their strengths need to be recognised and praised.

Write a story

Write a story about a five year old child coming to school with a certain health condition. Explain how this child will cope with this condition at school; what the school will need to provide and what teachers and children will do to make sure the child is fully included.

Ask the children to complete the Health Activity Sheet 2; share the responses with your class.

Find out at home

Choose a sportsperson, celebrity or someone they know who is overcoming a health condition and using it as stimulation to live a useful and purposeful life. Write about this person, how they have overcome obstacles and the kind of life they lead.

Eczema and other skin conditions – younger children

Circle Time

Sensitivity warning. If you have a child with eczema in your class you may wish to amend this activity.

Ask the children to roll up a sleeve and look at the skin on their arm. Ask them to examine this skin and to think of one thing they can say about it. Ask them to finish the sentence; 'My skin is...' Make a list of the things they say about their skin. Talk about how clever their skin is because it can mend itself if it gets scratched and close up if it gets a slit in it.

My skin is...

pink, brown, warm, shiny, slippery, soft, clean, hairy.

Explain to the children that some people have a skin condition called eczema or atopic dermatitis (AD). Their skin is not smooth and clear. It is often itchy and blotchy with patches of dry skin, sometimes inside their elbows and behind their knees. Children with eczema want to scratch their itchy skin and that makes it even worse. Ask the children how they think children who have eczema feel about their skin and make a list of these words, for example, upset, sad, shy.

Children who have eczema are often embarrassed about how it looks. Sometimes other children think it is 'catching' and that if they sit near them, their skin will go like that too. Help the children to understand that this is not true.

Tell a story

Grace was six and had eczema all over her legs and tummy. She couldn't have bubbles in her bath because these would irritate her skin. Her mum had to make sure she washed with special lotion as soap would make it feel even itchier and then she put special cream on the poor sore skin. Only Shona, Grace's best friend, knew about her eczema because Grace always wore trousers and long sleeves to school so that no one could see it. One day Toria caught sight of the sore and blotchy skin on Grace's ankle. 'Ugh,' she said. 'Look at Grace's skin, it's all horrid. Don't go near her or you'll get it; she's not playing with us.' Children crowded around and this made Grace want to cry. Shona went to help her. 'Don't be so horrid,' she said. 'It's not catching and it's bad enough to have eczema without you trying to exclude her.' And she put an arm around Grace. Two other children now felt badly about this and went to Grace and said it must be dreadful to have eczema. The teacher was listening and she called the class together and explained all about eczema. 'I'm proud of Shona,' she said. 'Shona's a real includer.' (Are you an includer like Shona?)

Eczema and other skin conditions – older children

Circle Time

Sensitivity warning. If you have a child with eczema in your class you may wish to amend this activity.

Ask the children whether any of them have skin problems and if so be sensitive to their feelings. Ask them all to examine their skin and to think about how they would describe it. Ask volunteers to describe their skin to the class. Ask them if they know about any of the problems that people can have with skin and if so to tell the class. These may include eczema, impetigo, acne, spots; some may mention leprosy. Many will have had painful sunburn at some time. Explain that sunburn in early childhood can cause skin damage that could be serious as people get older.

Explain about eczema and that, while in most cases this can not be cured, it can be controlled to some extent. Ask them to close their eyes and think about how they would feel if their skin was all itchy and flaky. Tell them that the more they scratch, the more it will itch. Skin conditions such as eczema are made worse because people are anxious or unhappy about them. Emotional feelings and those of inadequacy can cause worsening symptoms.

Explain that often young people in their early teens get spots because of hormone imbalance. These spots or acne are aggravated by scratching, squeezing or feeling embarrassed about them. They, or their friends, may well be affected in this way as they get older. It is important to make sure that those not affected help and support the others.

Ask the children to think how they would feel if they had a skin problem, spots or eczema and write a list of these feelings. Ask them to think how they would feel if they were excluded by others because of their poor skin; collect these feelings. Are the two lists the same?

What can you do?

Ask the children to think of all the things they can do to make sure they include people who have skin problems. Remind them that some people feel so badly about their skin that these feelings can actually make it worse. Ask them to make sure that they don't ever exclude people just because they have a skin condition.

Find out

Ask the children to find out about skin diseases, for example, athlete's foot, verrucas and also those that cannot be cured, such as psoriasis or leprosy. They will find out a lot of information if they put 'skin' into a search engine on the internet. In groups, ask each to choose one different skin problem to investigate and share their findings with the class.

Those who need a wheelchair – younger children

Tell a story

Zenda was only three years old when he had a dreadful accident. He was run over by a car and had to spend a lot of time in hospital. The doctors were worried that he would be paralyzed and not able to move at all, but after an operation they found he could move his arms and shoulders. His legs would not move at all. When he came out of hospital he was given a wheelchair so that he could get about and he soon learned to use this really well. When the time came for Zenda to go to school the doctors said he could go to an ordinary school as long as it was 'wheelchair friendly'. He started at the local school and soon had lots of friends. They all helped to include him in their games whenever they could. He knew that he would never be able to walk again but he had so many friends and helpers that he felt good about all the things that he could do even though he was disabled.

Talk about the story

Explain what 'disabled' means and that they are 'abled'. Explain what 'wheelchair friendly' means. Ask the children to tell you the things in your school that would make it easy for someone in a wheelchair to get about. Ask the children how they think they would feel if they couldn't walk. Talk about the things that people who can't walk can do for themselves. Do the children think that Zenda would like to be wheeled about or would he rather wheel himself? Would he like to be helped a lot or would he like to manage himself?

What could you do?

If someone in a wheelchair came to your school or classroom, what kinds of things could you do to make him feel good about himself? What kinds of things would you say to someone in a wheelchair about helping them? How would you say it to make sure they weren't hurt by the words you use?

A practical session

If at all possible ask someone in a wheelchair to come and talk to the children about the things that they can do and about how they like to be treated. Before the person comes, make sure that the children know how to say things in a way that would not hurt the person's feelings. It would be a good idea to write down the questions that the children can ask and check that the words are thoughtful and caring.

Disability Activity Sheet 1

You may like to first use the ideas from this sheet for discussion. Talk the children through it and after they have completed it, use their responses for discussion.

Those who need a wheelchair – older children

Disability Activity Sheet 2

Ask the children to do the activity sheet before starting on this work. Use their responses to generate discussion about being 'able-bodied' and 'disabled'. Discuss the need to be sensitive to the needs of a disabled person who may well not want help and prefer to show that he can do things himself.

I think a disabled person in a wheelchair would feel...

in control, sad, afraid, worried, miserable, happy, confident, able to do things, good at swimming, really strong arms, glad they could move around.

What can you do?

Ask the children to think of ways in which they can help children and others who are in a wheelchair. Ask them to work in small groups and make a list of 'Do's and Don'ts'.

A practical session

Most NHS wheelchairs are very basic and rely on arm power. Others and mobility scooters are powered by an electric battery and are much faster. If possible borrow a wheelchair from social services or the school nurse. It will probably be an NHS one. Let the children have practice in using it. They may be surprised at how difficult or easy it is to manoeuvre.

Wheelchair sports

Many disabled people have used their disability as a spur to show just what they can do.

Ask the children to think of all the sports that people who use a wheelchair can take part in. Make a list. Ask them to find out more by putting 'wheelchair' into a search engine; this will bring up 'wheelchair basketball' and many other sports.

Find out

Ask the children to find out about inspirational people who, despite being in a wheelchair, live a very active and productive life, people such as Swasie Turner, OBE. See www.swasieturner. org. Ask them to work in pairs to choose and find out about one person who is well known for their personality and achievements. The website http://lenmac.tripod.com/celebrities.html will produce a lot of information about various celebrities who are in wheelchairs.

Now that the children have found out about disabilities and disabled people, ask them to redo the activity sheet. Have their responses changed? Discuss these. Ask how many of them are an includer.

Health Activity Sheet 1

Here is a person with a short term health condition.
Draw yourself and write what you would say to them.

This person
has chicken pox.

I would say...

This is me...

This is a person with a permanent health condition.
What would you say to them?

This person
has type 1 diabetes.

I would say...

Turn over the paper and draw yourself back at school after being ill.
Write about your picture.

Unit 2

Health Activity Sheet 2

Draw a person with a short term health condition.
Write what it is and what you would say to them.

This person
has...

I would say...

Draw a person with a permanent health condition.
Write what it is and what you would say to them.

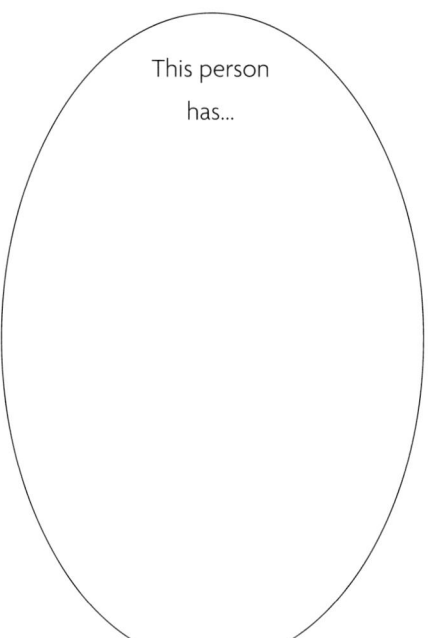

This person
has...

I would say...

Turn over the paper and draw yourself befriending someone with a permanent health condition.
Write what it is and what you would do to befriend this person.

Unit 2

Disability Activity Sheet 1

This is a disabled child who uses a wheelchair.	How do you think this person feels? I think...
Draw yourself talking to this person.	What could you do to help the person in the wheelchair? I could...

Turn over your paper and write about how you would feel if you were ill and had to use a wheelchair for a little while.

Disability Activity Sheet 2

Draw a disabled person.	How do you think this person feels about being disabled? What can they do and what can they not do?
Draw yourself with this person in school.	What can you say and do to help the disabled person to feel included in school life?

Turn over your paper and write about how you would feel if you were disabled and had to use a wheelchair.

Extension activities for younger children

Research

Ask the children if they know any people who are disabled. Can they tell them about the work they are doing at school and ask them to talk about how they feel about being disabled? Ask them to share the disabled person's comments at school.

Take home record sheet

Ask the children to make a record of one thing that they have learned during this unit that they didn't know before. Ask them to illustrate this record and to take it home to share with their family.

Investigation

Ask the children to take a good look at the shops in their shopping area. Are they all wheelchair friendly? How have some of the shops been adapted for wheelchair users? Could they do other things to make them better? Ask the children to write down what they find and discuss the findings at school.

Poster

Ask the children to work in pairs and devise a poster that would encourage everyone in the class to be a good includer. Initially ask them to draw the poster on A4 paper and share these with the class. Can you democratically choose one that could be enlarged for permanent display?

Privileged people

In Circle Time, explain to the children that some people are privileged and others are not. Sometimes there seems no reason for people to be rewarded for things they do and have.

Talk about the rewards you give to individual children.

- Do the children think these rewards are fair?
- Do all children have a chance to win them?
- How would children feel if they never won a reward?
- How would they feel if children were rewarded for poor work?

Being dumb

Help the children to experience the feeling of not being able to talk by insisting that they do not speak for a certain length of time, say 3 minutes the first time then increasing to longer if you think that they can do it! Explain that they can use all other methods of communication but not say a word.

Extension activities for older children

Research

Ask the children to find out all they can about the numbers of people in the UK with various disabilities. Leave this research open ended so that children will find out different data. Come together in the classroom and collate all the data into a chart about numbers of people with disabilities.

2

Take home record sheet

Write a list of all the parts in this unit on the board. Ask the children to use these as headings and to write a brief description of what they have learned from doing the work. Ask them to take their list home to share with their family.

Investigation

Ask the children to look at all the public buildings they visit outside school, for example, the library, the swimming pool, shops, petrol stations, country walkways. Ask them to write down how these have been made wheelchair friendly and to note any places where this is not so. Discuss what they can do about any non-wheelchair friendly places.

Poster

Ask children to design a poster that will make people stop, look and think about disability and how we should treat disabled people. It can be about any of the issues from this unit.

Privileged people

One morning, tell the children in the class that all people who have long hair are going to be privileged for the morning. Make sure that you identify these children; you could give them a badge or ribbon to wear. During the morning make sure that you give preferential treatment to this group of children. After lunch discuss how these children have felt all morning. Talk about how the other children have felt. Explain that this kind of discrimination is wrong but that it does happen. You may like to choose other privileged groups to give everyone a chance to know how it feels.

Being dumb

Ask the children to do the following activities without saying a word.
- Line up in order of height.
- Line up in order of birthdays.
- Those with house numbers, line up in order of their house number.
- Those with house names, line up in alphabetical order of house name.

Discuss how they felt, not being able to talk while they do this activity.

Reflect and remember

At the end of this unit talk about all the things the children have learned.

Remind them that you have all been learning about people who have disabilities or other health conditions and thinking about how to make sure they all feel included in life both in school and outside school.

Circle Time

Ask the children to think about one thing that they have learned and to finish the sentence:

'I have learned that...'

Ask the children to think about including children who are different in some way and to finish the sentence:

'One thing I can do to include children with health conditions is...'

Outside school

Discuss with the children the ways of relating to people outside school who have a health condition or disability. Remind them that people don't want pity; they want to be accepted into society as a valued member with skills and opportunities that can benefit us all.

It could be you

Remind the children of all the people who have battled against health and mobility difficulties and the perseverance that they have shown to learn new ways of coping.

Section 2
People with other conditions

Resources for this section on the CD-ROM:

Coloured posters for Unit 3 - Unit 8 and paired activity sheets.

Unit 3. Groups we belong to

How are we going to make sure we include new members in our group? Are we going to let new people in or try to exclude them? We want to make sure that all children understand the feelings of those rejected so that they can make sure that they don't reject or exclude others when they are secure in the group. We also want to make sure that the group is a positive entity and not used to discriminate or act against other members of society.

In this unit, after we consider the mores of belonging to family groups we look at various groups and settings under the following headings.

This unit is concerned with how we act towards children and others who are from a different group or setting to the one we are in.

- Families
- Games
- Sports
- Teams
- Different classes and schools
- Clubs.

There are paired activity sheets at the end of the unit.

Websites

http://www.wheelpower.org.uk/

http://www.paralympics.org.uk/

http://www.reddisability.org.uk/index-text-only/DisSport.htm

Families — *younger children*

Circle Time

Sensitivity warning. Be aware of any looked after children in your class.

Talk about families and how we are always part of this group, however small or large. Explain that families usually have rules, although these may not be written down rules. Ask them to think of their family's rules and finish the sentence: 'One rule in my family is...'

List some of these rules and try to discover how many of the same rules apply to lots of children's families.

> My family rules:
>
> Put your toys away.
> Put dirty clothes in the basket.
> Have a bath or shower every night.
> Clean your teeth.
> Don't hurt peoples feelings.
> Don't shout.
> Do your jobs with a smile.

Draw yourself in your family

Talk about the things they do in their family to make sure that people are happy and not sad or stressed; things such as caring for them, helping if they are tired, cheering them up if they are sad. Ask the children to draw themselves doing something in their family that shows they are helpful, kind or supportive to other members of the family. Help children to label their drawing or to write a sentence about it.

How does your family help you?

Ask the children to think about how the people in their family help them. What kinds of things do the people in their family do to show them that they care for them? Try to get children to move away from the toy buying idea and more towards the caring and loving role that parents and others take, for example, 'They read me stories,' or 'They help me to learn to ride my bike.' List all these on the board and ask the children to draw one of them. Cut out their drawings and write a caption alongside each about what is happening. Mount the drawings and captions on large backing paper with a heading such as: 'Things our families do to help us'.

What did you do?

Ask the children to think of a time when one of their adults was sad or unhappy. Ask them to think about what they did to cheer that person up. Ask volunteers to finish the sentence: 'When my... was sad, I...'

When things go wrong

Talk about how families help us if, or when, things go wrong. They are always there for us even if we have done something that is not so good. Remind the children that families forgive and include us.

Families Activity Sheet 1

Ask the children to complete the activity sheet to take home to show their family.

Families — older children

Sensitivity warning. Be aware of any looked after children in your class.

Discuss with the children the way that birds, animals and people have families to care for them and to help to bring them up. Explain that this is the basic group and the laws of nature intend that parents care for and nurture their young. In some cases there are no parents and others will step in to do this. Talk about animals on farms or in zoos where a parent is missing and another of the same, or different, species will do the nurturing. Can the children give you examples of this kind of thing?

Remind the children that as they grow older they will belong to other groups. What groups do they belong to now? What other groups will they want to belong to as they get older? For example, youth movements and sports groups. Explain that in this unit we will be looking at the rules and responsibilities of belonging to various groups but that for the moment we are thinking of family groups.

What we get from families

Talk about the kinds of support and comfort that humans receive from their families. Ask the children to give examples of when someone in a family did something out of the ordinary for another member of that family, for example, giving blood or an organ, taking in a family orphan. Ask the children to work in pairs and to write down a list of all the ways in which their families are supportive to them, with actual examples of what the family does or has done.

What we give to families

Remind the children that being in a family means giving as well as receiving and ask them to think of some of the things that they have been able to do for their family. Ask the children to work in small groups and draw up a list of examples of children helping or nurturing other members of their family.

Families Activity Sheet 2

Ask the children to complete this activity sheet to take home to share with their family.

Forgiving, accepting and including

There are families where members have become estranged for some reason. There may be current examples in the press of when family members have been re-united after several years. Estrangement usually starts with a simple argument or difference of opinion and if it is not resolved, this can go on for years. Some families have lost members due to conflict in their country. Discuss how this kind of thing can happen, how it could be prevented and what could be done to re-unite a family. You could extend this discussion by doing the research activity on the extension page at the end of this unit.

Ask the children to write a story of a re-inclusion of members of a family after they have been separated.

Games — younger children

Circle Time

Talk about the games that the children play. Some games need more than one player to make them work. Talk about group games and alone games.

Ask volunteers to tell you the games they like to play both at school and at home. Write these games on the board with the number of players alongside the name of the game. Ask the volunteers to tell the class the rules of the game and how it is played. Talk about what happens if people don't keep to the rules. Perhaps there are penalties or people have to miss a turn. Choose one board game that you have in the classroom and talk about its rules and what happens if people break them. Ask the children why it is important to keep to the rules of the game.

When I played snakes and ladders I had to keep going down snakes and it made me feel bad. Jagoda said it was a game and didn't matter and that cheered me up.

Excluding

Sometimes in games people are made to miss a turn or sit out and watch if they have made a mistake. Talk about how people feel then. Will the other players feel sorry for the one who is missing a turn or being excluded or will they not care? Ask the children to close their eyes and think of a time they were excluded from a game. How did they feel? How did they feel when they were back in the game again?

Tell a story

Alfons was choosing people to play a board game in the classroom and he didn't want George to play. He chose two other children. George felt really sad about this and he couldn't find anyone else to play with. He went and found a book to read and kept watching Alfons game. Sally said they ought to let George in because it was only fair to include him but Alfon's was in a strop and said, 'No.' Sally said that she wouldn't play then and went to join George. They talked for a bit and then began to play Snakes and Ladders.

Ask the children to tell you what they thought about Alfons. Was he a good includer? What about Sally? Ask them if there have been times when they didn't want to include someone in their game. What happened and how did they feel?

Ask the children to draw a picture and write about a time when they wanted to include someone in a game. Help them to write what happened.

Group and Alone Games Activity Sheet 1

Ask the children to complete this activity sheet. Collect in the papers and use what they have said in a later discussion.

Games We Can Play Activity Sheet 1

You may like to give the children this sheet to complete at home.

Games — older children

Ask the children to tell you the indoor games they play at home. Perhaps they play cards, Monopoly or other board games. Perhaps they play electronic games. Do they play these alone or do other people in the family join in? Do friends come to play? Do they like this or do they prefer to play with only some people? Ask them to tell you how they feel if people they don't like want to join in. What do they do?

My favourite game

Ask children to write about their favourite classroom game and to say how they would feel if they were excluded from playing it ever again. Discuss these responses.

Group or alone games

Discuss the advantages of group games and the advantages of alone games. How are the rules kept in both kinds of games? Is it easy to cheat in alone games? Does this make the game more interesting or does it lose something if you don't keep to the rules? After the discussion ask the children to complete the Group or Alone Games Activity Sheet 2.

Games for all

Ask the children to help you to make a list of the games you have in the classroom and a second list of games that children play at home. Ask the children to work in pairs and identify games, from both lists, that could be played by children with various disabilities or special needs. They can design their own grid for this or use the Games We Can Play Activity Sheet 2 at the end of this unit.

Including people in games

Explain that in a truly inclusive classroom all children should be able to join in all games and so some rules may have to be changed to make this possible. Ask volunteers to talk about games that might have to have changed conditions or rules so that everyone can play.

Design an inclusive game

Ask the children to think about designing a game that children with a disability could join in and play. Write a list of disabilities on the board and select one disability for each group of children.

This game has to be suitable for able-bodied children and also for children with the disability they have chosen. Perhaps children could adapt one of the games they have at home or at school so that it is suitable.

Give a short time for discussion, asking the groups of children to plan a game and its rules and to list all the materials they will need. Come together to talk about how each group of children can actually produce the game.

Ask the children, in their groups, to make a prototype of the game they have designed.

Sports — younger children

Circle Time

Talk to the children about the words 'sportsman' and 'sportswoman' and what they mean. Explain that as well as being someone who plays a game well, it also means someone who plays fairly and keeps to the rules. A true sportsperson would never want to exclude anyone for any reason.

Ask the children to volunteer to tell you the name of one sport and write these up on the board. Read through your list all together and then choose one game, asking volunteers to tell you how it is played or its rules.

Talk about each game and what you need to do to play it.

I can't see well.

I would like to play tennis but I wouldn't be able to see the ball I can play other games. I can play hopscotch.

What does a sportsperson need?

Ask the children to think of the qualities that people who play sports really need; make a list of these. Have they included 'practice' and 'determination' as well as having the kind of body that can do the sport?

Talk about people who would have difficulty in playing each sport on your list because of a disability and how they might feel about not being able to play it.

Tell a story

Gregor was seven years old and he loved playing football. One day while he was playing, he fell awkwardly and broke his leg. He had to go to hospital and have it set in plaster so that the bone would mend and be straight and strong. He couldn't play football for a very long time because even when the plaster came off he had to take care. It was summer time before he could play again and then it wasn't the football season. He had to wait until the autumn before play started again. He had been out of the game for a whole year.

Ask the children to say how they think Gregor felt when he couldn't play his favourite game. How would he feel when he was able to play again and it wasn't the season? How would he feel at the start of the autumn when the football season came round again?

Sports for everyone

Talk about some sports that disabled people can play equally with able-bodied people.

Sports — older children

Make a list

Ask the children to work in pairs and make a chart of six or more sports, listing the equipment and qualities a person needs in order to play that sport. They could use the Sports Activity Sheet 2 which has one sport done for them. Share these sport charts with the class and talk about the physical and personal qualities that the sportspeople need if they are to do each of the sports.

Can we include everyone?

Discuss this question.

Obviously there are many sports that disabled people cannot play depending on their kind of disability. Ask the children to think of sports that a disabled child in school may be able to play and whether the child will need special equipment or a relaxing of rules.

What do we mean when we say someone is a 'good sport'?

Ask the children to work in pairs to write a good definition of 'a sport'. Make a list of their responses and see if you can agree on one really good definition. Discuss sportsmanship. Do the children think that good sportsmanship would ever exclude anyone from playing?

Disabled sports

Talk about sports that disabled people can play on their own terms, for example, wheelchair basketball, rowing, swimming. Ask the children to find out at home about one sport that disabled people compete in. Share their findings at school and make a display listing all the sports they have discovered and the way disabled people compete in them.

Paralympic competitors

Ask the children to work in pairs to find out about the people who compete in these sporting events. Ask them to choose one sportsperson to find out about and to produce one page of A4 illustrated writing for you to discuss and display.

Find out at home, famous disabled sportspeople

Ask the children to find this website on the internet.

http://www.reddisability.org.uk/index-text-only/DisSport.htm.

Ask them to select one of the famous disabled sportspeople listed there and find out about this person's abilities. Ask the children to complete an A4 page of illustrated writing on their topic. You may like to make a display of the children's work with questions; try to link it to 'inclusion'.

Teams — younger children

Work teams or groups

Talk to the children about playing games or working in teams. Talk about occasions when you ask children to work as part of a group or team to find out about or work on a particular topic. Ask them to think of the advantages of working alongside others and to finish the sentence: 'I think working in a team is...'

Ask them now to think of any disadvantages of working as part of a team, for example, choosing a leader, waiting your turn, not being in charge, doing what other people want you to do.

After the children have had their say ask them to vote on whether they think working in a team is a good or not so good idea. Ask them to vote with their feet and move to one of three designated points in the room; 'Working as a team is always good', 'never good', 'sometimes good'. Ask volunteers from each group to explain their decision.

Sports teams in school

Talk about the need to work in teams in PE or sports. How are the teams chosen? Who does the choosing? How can you make sure the teams are equal? Do some people feel left out? How can this be avoided?

Can I be in your team?

Ask the children to think about times when they are playing a team game and someone else wants to join in. Is it always possible to let them? Are there times when it's not? Talk about good reasons for including people. If it's not possible to include someone, how would you say so without hurting the person's feelings?

What do you think?

Ask the children to do a piece of writing about team games and sports, whether in school or outside school. Ask them to illustrate their writing and to say whether they think team games are good or not.

Sports teams outside school

Talk with the children about local teams for sports. Do some of the children have favourite teams? How do they show which their team is; how do they support their team? Ask them to talk to their families about famous teams and to share this when back in school.

Teams – older children

What's your team?

Talk about the different kinds of sport teams, for example, football or basketball teams. Ask volunteers to talk about why they follow their favourite team. Discuss other sports and other kinds of teams, groups and partnerships, for example, tennis doubles partners, rowing teams.

Ask all the children to choose their favourite team or group and to write about why they chose this sports team and how they support it.

I support Manchester United. Their team is best. I wear the strip. It looks like this.

School teams

Most schools have various sports teams, for example, football or netball. Discuss how these teams are chosen. Do those who want to play have to show how good they are? Do they all practise together and then someone outside the class chooses the team? How is the choosing done?

Discuss the feelings of keen people who want to be in the team and who are not chosen. Is this fair? Could there be a second team with these participants? Could there be a changing team so that these players can be included?

Write a story

Ask the children to think of a story about someone who wanted to be in a school team and who was never chosen. Ask the children to make sure they discuss the feelings of all the people involved, the excluded player, as well as the person doing the choosing. Can they think of a good ending with the player being given a different role supporting the team?

Debate

Do we work better in the classroom if we are part of a team?

Discuss the above. Ask the children to tell you the pros and cons of working as part of a team or pair. Make a list of these; discuss each one.

Work together

Group the children into teams. Give them a practical task to organise, for example, make a cardboard box for a pair of shoes. Ask each team to submit a drawn plan and a list of materials; provide these. Set a starting time; time the groups. Discuss whether this was successful or not.

Different classes and schools – younger children

Circle Time

Ask the children to look around the class and see how many of the children went to their previous school or pre-school. Ask them to form a living graph by standing in a line with all the children that went to their previous school. Talk about these groups.

Four of the children from my last school are in this class. They are still my friends and I have some new ones.

Remind the children that being part of a group is like belonging to a family. Did they want to stick together when they came to your school? Did they want to exclude children who hadn't been in their previous school? Did they make new friends as well as their old friends? Ask volunteers to talk about their old and new friends.

Ask the children to think about their previous class before they came to your class. Ask them to close their eyes and think about the best thing they remember about their last class.

Ask them to finish the sentence; 'The best thing I remember about my last class is…'

Ask them to draw two pictures, one of their old classroom and one of this classroom and to draw some of the friends in each picture. Ask them to write about these friends.

New groups/old groups

Ask the children to think of the other children in their working group in your class. Ask them if they think this is like a new family? Do they miss the friends from their last working group? Do they still play together and are they still friends? Talk to the children about loyalty and what this means in terms of sticking by your friends. Ask the children to think of one occasion when they were loyal to an old friend. Ask volunteers to tell the group.

Tell a story

After a holiday Jason's teacher changed all the working groups and Jason was put in a group of eight with children he didn't know. At first, he felt sad about this as he missed his old friends, even though he could play with them at playtimes. He soon got to know his new group and he now had lots of friends. Sometimes his new group and his old friends didn't get on well together and this made Jason sad.

Ask the children these questions:

What would you say to Jason? What would you say to Jason's old and new friends?

Different classes and schools — older children

Circle Time

Discuss the various groups that you have in your class and school. Do the children move from group to group? Do they always work in the same groups? Do they work with children from other classes? Ask them to list the advantages and disadvantages of working with different groups of children.

> I have a new friend Jojo at school but I make sure that she joins in with my old friends. They would be hurt if I didn't still care for them.

Talk about friends and friendships. Ask the children to think of old friendship groups and new friendship groups. Do they overlap? Do they have friends they work with in the classroom and different friends in the playground?

Talk about what happens if friends from these two groups don't get on with each other.

Loyalty

Discuss the meaning of loyalty and how it applies to children in classes and schools. Discuss the difficulties of moving into other groups where they have new, different friends. Does this make them want to exclude old friends? If they want to do this, discuss how they can move on without hurting old friends.

Role-playing

Ask the children to work in groups of three. Tell them that you want them to role-play a friendship between two of them with one outside and to talk about how each of them feels. Ask them to change grouping with the outsider now one of the pair. Now how do they all feel? Change places again so that they have each had a time to role-play the one left out. Come together as a class and ask volunteers to say how they felt when they were in the pair of friends. Make a list of these feelings. Now ask them how they felt when they were the one left out. List these feelings. Talk about both sets of feelings.

Debate

Ask the children to think of how friendship groups change and to focus on:

- moving on and leaving some friends behind
- keeping groups of friends separate
- sharing friends from different groups
- thinking of friends' feelings when moving on.

Ask them to write about changing friends without excluding old friends.

Clubs — younger children

Circle Time

Ask the children to think about any clubs or outside school groups that they belong to. Ask volunteers to name these and make a list. Talk about the friends they may have in these clubs; do they have school friends and club friends or do some overlap?

Overlapping circles

Ask the children in one of your working groups to each write their name on a small piece of paper while you write the name of their group on a piece of paper. Place two hoops in the centre of the circle, making them overlap. Put the name of the working group inside one hoop and ask the children to place their names also in that hoop. Ask one of these children to tell you the name of a club or group they belong to; write the group's name on a piece of paper and put it in the other hoop. This second hoop has no members yet, neither does the overlap. Ask children whose names are in the first hoop to move them to the overlap if they belong to both groups. Ask which children from the class also belong to the second group and explain that their names would go in that circle.

Ask all the children to draw around discs on paper to make overlapping circles and inside each circle to write the names of two groups they belong to. Ask them to draw pictures of the people who belong in each group, putting those who belong to both groups in the overlap. Ask volunteers to talk about these two groups of friends; in particular how they manage these friendships so that no one feels left out. You might like to use the Overlapping Circles Activity Sheet 1 for this activity.

Tell a story

Amran was seven years old and he belonged to a swimming club. Some boys from his class at school also belonged to the club. They went every Friday afternoon after school. When it was Amran's birthday he invited some friends from school and some from the swimming club who were not at the school. When they were going to sit down for the birthday tea some squabbles broke out because children from one group didn't want to sit next to children from the other group. They thought they were more Amran's friends than the others. Amran was annoyed and shouted, 'You're all my friends, I like you all equally.'

Ask the children what they would say to Amran, the school friends and the swimming friends.

How could Amran make sure that both sets of friends felt equally valued and included?

Clubs Activity Sheet 1

Talk about clubs that can and can not include disabled people. Talk through this activity sheet with the children and ask them to complete it.

Clubs — older children

Ask the children to work in small groups and produce a list of all the clubs and outside school groups that are in your area. Make one list from all these and write it up in some kind of order, for example, alphabetically or 'physical' and 'non-physical' groups. Ask children to tell you which clubs or groups they belong to and write the number of children alongside it. Discuss what qualifications children need in order to belong to these clubs, for example, whether they need to be proficient in anything or of a certain age. Discuss whether these clubs and groups are exclusive or inclusive. If some people are excluded from joining are there valid reasons?

Exclusion

Ask the children to think how children would feel if they were not allowed to join a group or club that their friends had joined. Some restrictions may require that children have reached a certain level in a sport or activity; others may require the child's body to be of a certain strength. Ask the children to work in pairs and, using the list of clubs on the board, identify those that have restrictions and discuss whether these are fair.

Ask them to make a chart, listing each club or group, adding alongside any exclusions. Come together as a class and discuss these charts.

Children with disabilities or special needs

As a class, using your list of groups and clubs, identify all those that would be able to cater for children with disabilities or special needs. Make another column alongside the list on the board and write in this column those that are fully inclusive.

How would you feel?

Ask the children to think about how they would feel if they were unable to join a certain club for some reason. Ask volunteers to say how they would feel and write up these 'feelings' words on the board.

Clubs Activity Sheet 2

Ask children to complete the first part of the activity sheet.

Debate

Ask the children to write down their feelings about the two statements on the Clubs Activity Sheet 2. Ask them to form two groups; one that agrees with the first statement and the other that agrees with the second. Ask each group to organise a spokesperson to speak about their statement. Ask the class to finish their activity sheet and then to vote on which sentence they think is the truest.

Overlapping Circles Activity Sheet 2

Use this activity sheet either in class or as a homework activity. Discuss the difficulties in maintaining good friendships.

Families Activity Sheet 1

My name is..

Think of three things that you do in your family to help others.

Draw what you do.	Write what you are doing.

Turn over.

Draw your family being happy because you are doing something for them.

Families Activity Sheet 2

My name is..

What we get from our families.

What we give to our families.

Turn over.

Draw all the people who live in your home and write one sentence about each person.

Group and Alone Games Activity Sheet 1

My name is...

Write down the names of two group games you know.

1.

2.

Write down the good things about group games.

The good things about group games are...

Write down the names of two alone games you know.

1.

2.

Write down the good things about alone games.

The good things about alone games are...

Turn over the paper and draw yourself playing a group game and an alone game.
Which do you like best?

Unit 3

Group and Alone Games Activity Sheet 2

My name is..

Group Games	
The advantages of group games are...	The disadvantages of group games are...

Alone games	
The advantages of alone games are...	The disadvantages of alone games are...

Turn the paper over.

Write down the rules of one group game, its advantages and disadvantages. Write down the rules of one alone game, its advantages and disadvantages.

Unit 3

Games We Can Play Activity Sheet 1

My name is...

A person playing tennis.	
  	This game is called...
Who is this game suitable for?	
Who is this game not suitable for?	
Draw your picture of a person playing a different game.	Name of the game.
Who is this game suitable for?	
Who is this game not suitable for?	

Turn over the paper and draw yourself playing a game. Write about your picture.

Unit 3

Games We Can Play Activity Sheet 2

My name is...

Picture of person playing the game	Name of game	Who is this game suitable for?	Who is this game not suitable for?

Turn over your paper and draw a disabled person playing a game. Write about your picture.

Sports Activity Sheet 1

My name is...

Draw a disabled person playing a non-disabled sport.	Write what this sport is and what the disabled person needs to be able to play it.
Draw a disabled person playing a sport for disabled people to play.	What is this sport and how is it played?

Turn over the paper. Draw yourself playing a sport with a disabled person. Write how you feel playing sport with someone who is disabled and write how the disabled person feels.

Unit 3

Sports Activity Sheet 2

My name is...

Name of sport	Equipment needed	Qualities of player
Tennis	a court racquets and balls instruction book or coach.	fast footwork a good eye for the ball a strong arm.

Turn over the page.

Draw yourself playing your favourite sport. Write what it is. Can any disabled people play this sport? What disabilities could someone have and still be able to play this sport?

Overlapping Circles Activity Sheet 1

My name is ....

Think of two groups you belong to and write their names in each circle.

Draw yourself in the overlap. Think of people who belong to one or both of the groups. Draw each person once in either of the circles or in the overlap.

Turn over the paper. Write about how you make sure you are good friends to people in both groups.

Overlapping Circles Activity Sheet 2

My name is ....

Think of three groups you belong to and write their names in each circle.

Draw yourself in the overlap. Think of the people who belong to one or both of the groups. Write each person's name once in the correct circle or in the correct overlap.

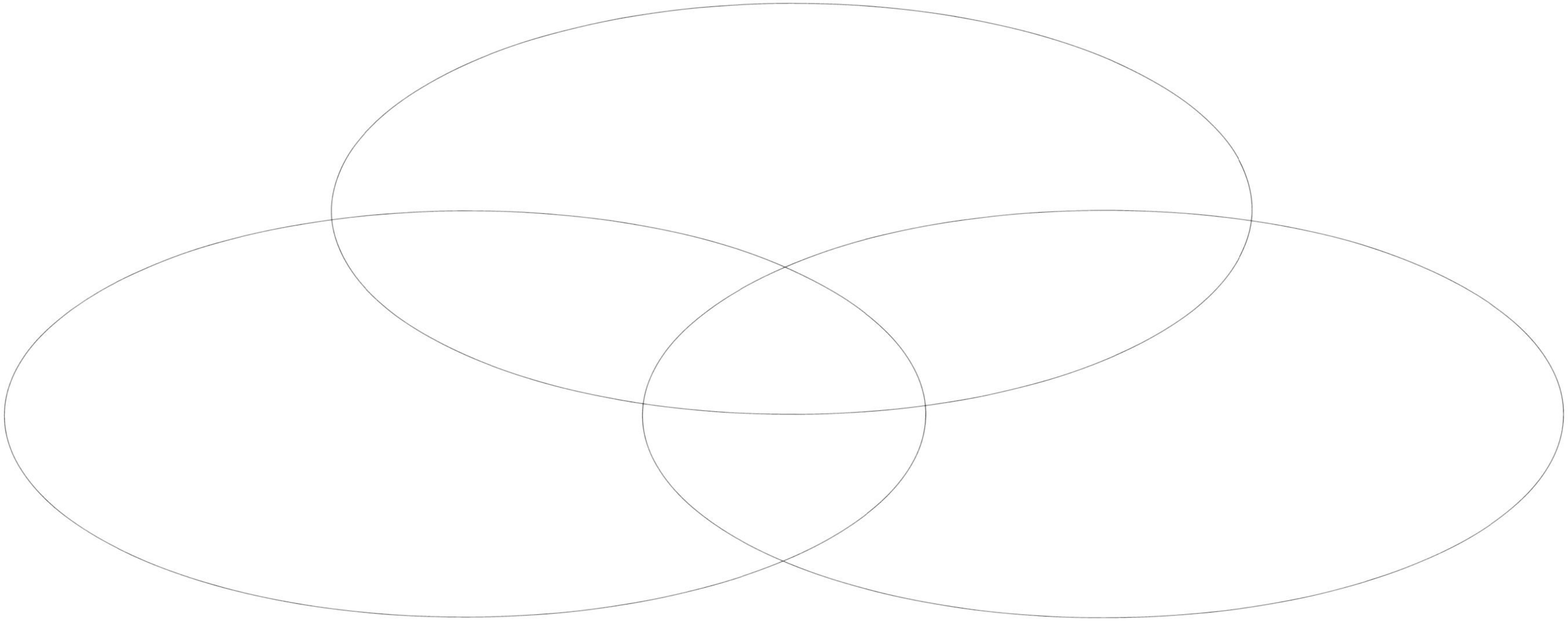

Turn over the paper. Write about how you manage these friendships so that no one is left out.

Clubs Activity Sheet 1

My name is..

Think of two different kinds of after school clubs.

Draw someone in each club, write about what people do there. Then write underneath whether children with disabilities could join in or not.

This club is...	Children at this club...

Disabled children could/could not join in this club because...

This club is...	Children at this club...

Disabled children could/could not join in this club because...

Turn over your paper.

Draw and write about a club that disabled children could join.

Clubs Activity Sheet 2

My name is ....

Write your responses to the statements in Part 1 before the debate and do Part 2 after the debate.

Part 1. Before the debate.
I think all clubs should be fully inclusive of all children because...
•   •   •
I think all clubs can never be fully inclusive of all children because...
•   •   •
Part 2. After the debate.
I think that...

Turn over the paper.

Write down some of the points that people made in the debate.

Extension activities for younger children

Research

Ask the children to talk to their families about living members of their family who are no longer in the close family circle. They may be people who have moved to another town and have lost close contact. Some may have a roving occupation. Ask volunteers to share what they have discovered with the whole class.

Research

Ask the children to find out if any of their ancestors emigrated to another country to seek a new life there. Are any of the children in contact with these relatives? If so ask volunteers to talk about this and about how they keep in touch. Repeat the process for immigrants.

Take home record sheet

Ask the children to make a record of one thing that they have learned during this unit that they didn't know before. Ask them to illustrate this record and to take it home to share with their family.

Investigation – what do people know about sports for disabled?

Ask the children to talk to their families, friends at home and friends from other classes in the school to find out what sports and games they know about that disabled people can play. Ask the children to make a list of these sports and games; talk about them in class and make one complete list. Do the children in your class know more about these than the people they have surveyed?

Poster

Ask the children to work in small groups to make a large poster telling people about the kinds of sports and games that disabled people can do. Ask them to put drawings of people playing these games and sports on their posters. Display all the posters around the school.

Group task

Explain that you want them to work in groups to make a building out of junk materials, glue and sellotape. Allow each group a few minutes to talk about how they will do this. Help the children to assemble the materials they choose to use and explain that they can only have ten minutes to do this.

Signal the start of the task.

Signal the end of the task.

Ask children to look at all the buildings that have been constructed before coming together as a group.

Ask volunteers from each group to talk about the difficulties of working together to make this building. Ask volunteers to talk about the advantages of working in a group.

Extension activities for older children

Research

Write 'families reunited' in a search engine on the internet and read some of the stories of how families have found each other again. Working in small groups ask them to choose one of the stories to report to the whole class.

Research

Ask the children to find out about wheelchair sports. They will find the following website useful:

http://www.wheelpower.org.uk/

Ask the children to make a list of four wheelchair sports and to describe how the sport is played.

Take home record sheet

Write a list of all the parts in this unit on the board. Ask the children to use these as headings and to write a brief description of what they have learned from doing the work. Ask them to take their list home to share with their family.

Investigation

Ask the children to talk to the organisers of any club or group to which they belong. Ask them to investigate the possibilities of disabled people being allowed to take part in that club or group and to find out which people can be included and which can not be included. Ask the children to make a written report of this investigation for later discussion at school.

Poster

Ask the children to imagine a new club or group that is especially for disabled children. Ask them to work in small groups, choose a name for the club and list the activities on offer for the disabled children. Ask them to design an illustrated poster for this imaginary club inviting able-bodied people to help to organise and run it.

Group task

Explain that you want them to build a free standing structure using only newspaper and sellotape.

- Organise the class into groups of four or five children.
- Give three minutes discussion time.
- Allow five minutes construction time.

Ask children to visit each construction and discuss the success or otherwise of each group's construction.

Give each group five minutes to discuss how they could make their construction bigger or better and ask a spokesperson to tell the class about this.

You could repeat this exercise at a later date using the same groups.

Reflect and remember

At the end of this unit talk about all the things the children have learned.

Remind them that you have all been learning about:

- belonging to certain groups

- considering who is permitted to belong

- whether it is possible for all children, regardless of their physical or mental abilities, to be included.

Circle Time

Ask the children to think about one thing that they have learned from their work in this unit and to finish the sentence: 'I have learned that...'

Outside school

Discuss with the children the ways of relating to children in groups inside and outside school who have a health condition or disability.

Remind them that all children have something to offer; they all want to be accepted into society as a valued member.

It could be you

This unit has been concerned with how we act towards children and others who are in a different group or setting to the one we are in.

- We have thought about making sure we include new members to the group.

- We have tried to understand the feelings of those rejected, to make sure that we don't reject others when we are secure in a group, rather seek to find ways we can include them.

Ask the children if they think they are good includers.

Unit 4. Nationality, religion, socio-economic difference

In a multi-cultural society it is important to integrate all people. Children need to concern themselves about how to integrate and include all members of society with no exclusions at all.

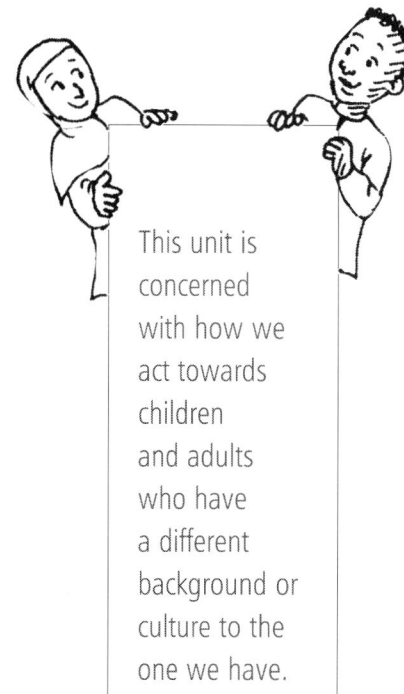

This unit is concerned with how we act towards children and adults who have a different background or culture to the one we have.

We want to help children to understand the feelings of rejection and exclusion so that they will make sure they are not a party to this. We also want to make sure that small groups of children do not feel set apart from the general classroom society and are never, in any way, discriminated against.

You may like to view this unit of the book as a starter for this topic as it is a very sensitive area. You may wish to pursue it, depending on the children in your school and class and any concerns you may have about children including others in their work and play.

The headings are:

- Nationality
- Religion
- Socio-economic groups.

There are activity sheets at the end of the unit.

Useful websites

http://www.omsakthi.org/religions.html

http://www.krysstal.com/borrow.html

4

Nationality — younger children

Circle Time

Talk with the children about other countries that they may have visited and make a list of these. Go through the list, one by one, asking children who have visited there to tell you two things about that country. Put their comments alongside the name of the country.

Ask the children to think of how the people look who live in or have come from these countries. Ask volunteers to finish the sentence: 'The people from... (name of country) look..'

The people from China have very black hair.

In this country

Talk to the children about how people from different nationalities may feel when they come to visit or live in this country. What kinds of things will they find different, for example, the weather, the shops, the houses, the jobs people do, the schools. If you have children from different nationalities in your class ask them if they would like to tell you all about the country where their ancestors lived.

In This Country Activity Sheet 1

Explain how the children can complete this activity sheet. When they have all finished, talk about what they have drawn and written.

How do they feel?

Ask the children to think about how people from other countries feel when they visit our country. Will they feel comfortable among people from so many different nationalities? Will they feel different? Ask the children how they feel when they visit other countries and to finish the sentence: 'When I visit other countries I feel...'

Fitting in

Ask the children to think of a child and his parents coming to live in this country from far away. Talk about how they will feel if there are lots of people from their country living near to them. How might they feel if there are no people from their country living near them?

What can we do?

Talk about what your children can do when someone from another country comes to be in your class. What kinds of things can they do to make sure they welcome this child and make them feel valued and included, for example, be friendly, play with them at games, help them to know about your school, sit by them and get to know them?

Nationality — older children

Remind the children that this country has a multi-cultural society and that people from all over the world have come to live here over many centuries. Can they give examples of other nationalities that have settled here in the past, for example, the Romans, the Normans, the Flemish weavers who settled in Norfolk in the 12th Century and established the wool industry?

Language

Explain that the language we think of as English consists of many words from other languages, for example,
- blizzard (from USA)
- sauce (from France)
- bungalow (from India)
- fjord (from Norway)
- patio (from Spain).

Ask the children to find out six or more words that we use in English that have originated from other countries and nationalities. (You can allow then to cheat by giving them the website http://www.krysstal.com/borrow.html)

Make a data line

Ask the children whether they think that people coming to live in this country will find it easy or hard to settle here. Ask them to make a data line, with one end of the line being 'easy' and the other being 'hard', with 'half and half' in the middle. Ask volunteers to give reasons for their position in the data line.

In This Country Activity Sheet 2

Ask the children to complete this activity sheet and when they have done this, use their responses as a basis for a discussion.

What can people do?

Discuss with the children what people in this country can do to help families from other nationalities to settle here.

What can you do?

Discuss with the children what they can do to help children from other nationalities to settle:
- in your school
- in your neighbourhood
- in this country.

Write a story

Ask the children to write a story about a family coming to live in this country and to say what was easy and what was difficult; were they included in the life of the community?

Religion — younger children

Circle Time

Explain to the children that the word 'religion' usually means a way of living according to a faith or belief of the rules set down by its founder. In this country most of the people are Christians but people from other nationalities have their own religions, for example, Judaism and Hinduism. (You may like to find out how many religions are represented in your class.)

Who do we worship?

Each religion has a god or gods that its people worship. This is usually a holy person who lived a good life and who has left a set of rules for its people to live by. Christians worship God or Jesus Christ and many believe that Mary, mother of Jesus is a holy woman. Other religions worship different gods.

Where do we worship?

People usually worship their god or gods in some special building; these may be churches, mosques, synagogues or temples. Explain that people from some religions don't have a place of worship; sometimes they worship outside or in people's houses.

Can anyone join in?

Talk to the children about belonging to a church or religion. Explain that children usually belong to the church where there parents go and that they are accepted as a full member of the religion after taking some training. Most religions are happy to accept new members and will make it easy for new people to be included and to become a full member of it.

Is anyone excluded?

It is not normal for anyone to be excluded from joining a religion and worshipping in its place of worship in this country. In some countries, people are forbidden to go to certain religious places. People from some countries have had to leave their homes if they want to worship the god of their choice.

Celebrations

All religions have their ceremonies and celebrations. Talk to the children about religious festivals in your area. Do some religions have carnivals or processions? Ask the children to tell the class of any of these that they have attended.

This is me at the Notting Hill Carnival.

Religion – older children

Discussion

Ask the children if they can explain in their own words what religion is.

You may like to use the definition below from Wikipedia online

> 'A religion is a set of common beliefs and practices generally held by a group of people, often codified as prayer, ritual, and religious law. Religion also encompasses ancestral or cultural traditions, writings, history, and mythology, as well as personal faith and mystic experience. The term 'religion' refers to both the personal practices related to communal faith and to group rituals and communication stemming from shared conviction.'

Freedom to worship

Explain that in this country people are free to choose their religion and to worship the god of their choice. It was not always so in this country and even now in some countries people are not allowed to practise certain religions. Discuss persecution of Roman Catholics in this country in the time of Henry VIII. You could link this to the persecution of the Jews in Nazi Germany.

Religious unrest

Discuss current unrest in other countries where the underlying cause is often religion. Do the children know that people have often left their own country because they want to worship in a way that is forbidden by the leaders of the country? Do they know that governments of some countries are persecuting people of certain religions? Do they know that, in leaving their own country, many people have become refugees in Western countries? Discuss the 'exclusion' angle of this.

Freedom of choice

Explain that in this country we have freedom to choose our religion and to worship as we please. No one is left out. Most religions accept new members as long as they agree to learn about the religion and to practise in the recognised way. There are many religions in this country and many different kinds of places of worship. Make a list of the ones you know.

Find out and write

Ask the children to find out and write about one religion from the list. Ask them to illustrate their writing. Share this writing with the class. Emphasise that most religions in this country are not exclusive and that everyone may join in.

4

Socio-economic groups – younger children

Circle Time

Sensitivity warning. Be aware of differences between rich and poor children in your class.

Talk with the children about the differences between families; some families are very big, some are small; some have lots of children, some have few; some have pets, some do not; some are rich and live in big houses, others are very poor and live in very small homes. Explain that in between there is a great variety of homes where some children have a lot of possessions and some have few.

Tell a story

Zak lives with his mother. He has no father and no brothers and sisters but he has a dog called Jasper. Jasper is very big and very black and Zak loves him very much. Raphael has just come to live with his three brothers in a big house in the next street. Raphael's mother and father both work and so the children are often looked after by their granny. Jasper wishes that he had brothers and lived in a big house. Raphael wishes that he had a dog.

Ask the children to answer these questions and then do the Zak and Raphael Activity Sheet 1 at the end of this unit:

Is Zak happier than Raphael because he has a dog?
Is Raphael happier than Zak because he has a big family and lives in a big house?
Can Zak include Raphael in his circle of friends? How will he do this?

Talk about it

Ask the children to think about a child from a wealthy family who has all the latest stuff, for example, the latest toys or clothes. Would they include this child in their circle of friends? If so, why? If not, why not?

Ask the children to think about a child coming to their school with very poor clothes and no nice toys. Would they like to be friends with this child? If so, why? If not, why not?

A big change

Ask the children to write a story about a girl who lives with her family in a very small flat with few toys and rarely any outings. She has lots of friends. The family win the lottery and now have lots of money. What will happen to the girl and her friends now? Will she still be friends with her old friends? Will she go to a new posh house and school and want new friends? Will she include or exclude people from her old life? Share the stories.

Sleepover Activity Sheet 1

Ask the children to complete this and then talk with them about their solutions. Remind the children that it is not what we have that is important, but what we are.

Socio-economic groups — older children

Explain to the children that socio-economic means the different strands in society. These used to be according to whether people were rich or poor. Nowadays socio-economic groups are graded by the work that the wage earners do. People with well paid jobs tend to live in big houses and have a lot of money. People who work in low paid jobs or are unemployed do not have much money and tend to live in poorer areas.

Talk with the children about the 'haves' and the 'have nots' in our society. Ask the children if there are problems when children who have a lot of things have friends who do not have many things. What could these problems be? How could children overcome them?

> I think it is better to have friends and no toys because you can always make up games and make toys but you can't do without friends.

Debate

'Is it better to have friends but no toys or no friends and lots of toys?'

Take a vote.

Examine this situation

In one class at primary school there were three separate friendship groups. One group were children who came from a posh housing estate; they went horse-riding and skiing and belonged to a gym club. Another group were children from a poor estate who didn't have many outings or holidays. The third group were children from parents who both worked and so they belonged to an after-school group. These three groups of children were really very separate; they didn't work or play well together. The teacher wanted to find ways to help them to mix better and for them to include people from other groups.

Ask the children to work in pairs to suggest ways in which these children could be encouraged to work together.

Suggest a good outcome

Jaxon was a new boy in the class. He came from a private school where he had to wear a posh uniform and where there were small classes. He felt really out of things when he started at their school. He had no friends and couldn't get on with the kind of work they did in their class. No one wanted to be his friend, so he was excluded from all groups. The children said he was a 'snob' and wouldn't let him join in. The teacher didn't seem to be able to help him.

Ask the children to work in pairs to suggest solutions to this problem.

Sleepover Activity Sheet 2

Ask the children to complete this; talk with them about their comments.

In This Country Activity Sheet 1

My name is ....

Jerzy is Polish and has come to live in this country. His name means earth worker or farmer. He will find some things the same and some things different.

What things will be the same?

This is a picture of Jerzy.

What things will Jerzy find are different in this country?
The first one has been done for you.

Jerzy will find some foods are different from foods in Poland.

Jerzy will find...

Jerzy will find...

Jerzy will find...

Turn over the paper. Draw a picture of you and Jerzy playing together. Write what you are doing.

Unit 4

In This Country Activity Sheet 2

My name is..

Radko has come from Bulgaria to live in this country. His name means happy. Think about the things he will find easy in this country and write three of them down.

This is a picture of Radko.

Radko will find these three things easy:

1. I think he will find this easy because...

2. I think he will find this easy because...

3. I think he will find this easy because...

Now think of three things Radko will find difficult.

1. I think he will find this difficult because...

2. I think he will find this difficult because...

3. I think he will find this difficult because...

Turn over the paper and write some good advice to Radko that will help him to settle in this country and to feel included.

Then write what you could do to help Radko if he came to your school and class.

Zak and Raphael Activity Sheet 1

My name is..

Draw Zak, Raphael and Jasper.

I think Zak will want to be friends with Raphael because...

I think Raphael will want to be friends with Zak because...

Turn over the paper and draw you with some friends. Does it matter if they have more things than you have? Write your answer.

Zak and Raphael Activity Sheet 2

My name is...

Zak and Raphael have written to an agony aunt. What would you write in reply if you were the agony aunt?

Dear Agony Aunt,

I live with my mother in a small flat. I have a dog called Jasper. We don't have much money and I can't have many things *because* Mum doesn't have a big wage.

My problem is that I would like to be friends with Raphael *but* he has lots of toys and lots of money. How can I *ask* him to be my friend and come to visit me in our little flat?

Yours sincerely,

Zak

Dear Zak,

Dear Agony Aunt,

I've just moved with my family to a *big* new house. I have three brothers and *because* both my parents work, Granny comes to look after us after school. I don't know any children here yet and have no friends. There is a boy at school called Zak and I would like to have him as a friend *but* he lives in a little flat with just his mother and a lovely dog; they don't have much money.

My problem is that I would like to play with him *but* it could be difficult *because* we come from different backgrounds. What shall I do?

Yours sincerely,

Raphael

Dear Raphael,

Turn over your paper and write about a day in the lives of Zak and Raphael as they decide to become friends.

The Sleepover Activity Sheet 1

My name is..

Sarah wanted Jill and Dita to come to her house for a sleepover. Jill said she didn't want to come if Dita came because she didn't like Dita, who came from a poor Polish family. Sarah didn't know what to do because she liked both girls. How do you think everyone felt?

Draw Sarah, Jill and Dita.

I think that Sarah felt...

I think that Jill felt...

I think that Dita felt...

What is the best thing for Sarah to say and do?

I think Sarah should...

Turn over the paper and write two different endings to this situation.
One good ending for Sarah and one good ending for Dita.

Unit 4

The Sleepover Activity Sheet 2

My name is ....

Twins, Masie and Bron were having a sleepover birthday party. They could invite five friends to come. One of the friends called Zoë wouldn't come because her special friend wasn't invited. The twins didn't invite Zoë's friend because she came from a poor family.

How did everyone feel?

I think that the twins felt...

I think that Zoë felt...

I think that Zoë's friend felt...

The twins' parents weren't sure what to do about this party. What would you say to them?

I would say...

Turn over the paper and write a story about someone being excluded because of where they live. Give two endings to the story, a good one and a not so good one.

Extension activities for younger children

Research

Long ago when people came to this country they brought things from their own country with them, for example, potatoes, tobacco, weaving skills, cuisine, festivals. Ask the children to work as a group and find out one item that people brought with them. As soon as each group has decided on their item ask them to write this on the board so that other groups will choose a different item.

Ask the children to write up their findings with illustrations and to say how we have included their item in the life of this country. Make a display to share this work.

Take home record sheet

Ask the children to make a record of one thing that they have learned during this unit that they didn't know before. Ask them to illustrate this record and to take it home to share with their family.

Investigation

Ask the children to talk to their families about any special foods that they have in their family. For example, do they have special birthday cakes or unusual foods for other special occasions?

Ask them to find out and write about other family or religious celebrations. Discuss all these findings in Circle Time.

Artwork

Discuss all the things the children have discovered about what people have brought to this country from their own and list these. Ask the children to draw one or two of these. Cut them out and use them to make a collage. Decide on a title for the collage and use speech bubbles to label and explain what the pictures represent.

Drama

Group the children in pairs. Ask them to take on the role of someone coming to this country and someone welcoming and including them. Allow only three minutes before changing over. Have a short discussion before asking volunteers to show their role-play to the class.

Language activity

Ask the children to work in pairs, choose a language and learn a useful phrase from this language, for example, 'Hello', 'Please', 'Thank you', 'Can you help me?' With very young children you could choose one language and help them all to learn a phrase or two. Use these phrases in your everyday teaching.

Extension activities for older children

Research

Ask the children to work in pairs to find out about people from one other nationality who came to this country long ago and settled here. Ask them to find out what these people brought to this country and how their skills and language have enriched the culture here. Ask the children to identify any physical, social or cultural differences of the nationality they choose to research. Ask each pair to make an illustrated data sheet of their findings and display these for everyone to see.

Take home record sheet

Write a list of all the parts in this unit on the board. Ask the children to use these as headings and to write a brief description of what they have learned from doing the work. Ask them to take their list home to share with their family.

Language investigation

Ask the children to use dictionaries, the internet and family to find out the source of a set of new or slang words that you give them. You could use words such as:

- posh
- slob
- Sloan Ranger
- Essex girl
- wicked.

Ask children for other words that they know, such as texting shortcuts, internet slang and emoticons such as :-) and :o(. Discuss and/or make a list of these.

Religious festivals

Ask the children to help you to make a list of all the religious festivals you and they know. Ask them to add to this list by using books, families and the internet. Working in pairs, ask children to find out and write an illustrated piece about one or more of these. Use their combined work to make a wall display.

Posters

Ask the children to work in small groups to design a poster about inclusion of people from different nationalities, religions and socio-economic groups. Ask for rough prototype work on A4 and then discuss ways to improve them and check the words they have used. Ask them to enlarge their posters to A3 size for display.

Reflect and remember

This unit has been about helping children to understand the feelings of rejection and exclusion that can happen because of nationality, religion or various socio-economic groups so that they will make sure they are not a party to this. We also want to make sure that small groups of children do not feel set apart from the general classroom society and are never, in any way, excluded or discriminated against.

At the end of this unit talk about all the things the children have learned. Remind them that you have all been learning about people who come from different groups of society and thinking about how to make sure that all are included, no matter what their nationality, religion or socio-economic group.

Circle Time

Ask the children to think about one thing that they have learned from their work in this unit and to finish the sentence: 'I have learned that...'

Outside school

Remind the children that it is up to them to relate to, and include, people from various groups outside school. They need to concern themselves about how to integrate and include all members of society with no exclusion at all. Discrimination against anyone, for whatever reason, is not only unkind but can have far reaching consequences.

It could be you

Remind the children that within society they could find that they are the one left out. A good includer would accept and include all members of society no matter what their nationality, religion or to which socio-economic group they belong.

Unit 5. Speech and language differences

We really want all children to understand, feel empathy for and include children with speech problems or different accents, whether from this country or from a different country.

This unit is concerned with how we act towards children and others who speak in a different way from most children in their setting.

You may well not have any children in your class or school with speech problems or different accents but it is important to help the children to understand both how children with difficult or different speech may feel and how they themselves should react to them.

In this unit, we will be considering children who speak differently from most of the children in the class under the following headings.

- Speech impairment
- Stammer
- Foreign accents
- Regional accents.

Useful websites

To see videos of deaf children who are learning to speak, visit:

http://www.oraldeafed.org/movies/index.html

Visit this website to see pictures and writing done by children who have a stammer.

http://www.stammertrust.co.uk/pdf/drawings.pdf

This website has audio clips of various regional accents.

http://www.collectbritain.co.uk/collections/dialects/

http://www.literacytrust.org.uk/Database/stats/EALstats.html#20languages

http://en.wikipedia.org/wiki/List_of_languages_by_first_written_accounts#Before_1000_BC

http://en.wikipedia.org/wiki/Language#Formal_languages

http://surnames.behindthename.com/

http://www.cockneyrhymingslang.co.uk/slang/apples_and_pears

Speech impairment – younger children

Explain that sometimes young children start school with some kind of speech impairment. This may make it difficult for others to understand what the child says. Sometimes the child's speech will get better as the child gets older; some children may need to receive help from a speech and language specialist.

Circle Time

Talk to the children about speech impairment and how a baby's speech develops. Explain that sometimes a baby's words are funny and became part of the family history. Ask them if they can remember saying some words wrongly or using the wrong words when they were young. Ask volunteers to finish the sentence: 'When I was young, I used to say...'

Tell a story

Roslyn was starting school and she had a speech impairment. She couldn't say some sounds and the words came out wrong. In her new classroom there were some children who were rather unkind and on the very first day they mocked and mimicked Roslyn's speech. This made her very unhappy and she told her mum that she didn't want to go to school ever again, because she didn't feel one of the group at all.

Roslyn is in my group. She is happy with us all. We take care of her.

Ask the children what Roslyn's Mum could have said and done.

Ask them to say what Roslyn's teacher could have done.

Ask them to say what they could have said or done if they were in Roslyn's class. Would that help Roslyn to feel included?

Finish the story

Ask the children to think of a good ending to Roslyn's story. Ask them to draw a picture of the ending and write what happened.

New words

Choose some new words your children will not yet have met; words that are hard to pronounce. You may like to choose words from another language. Tell the children that you are going to play a remembering game and ask them to remember two or three of these words. Give them only one chance to repeat the words after you, calling them word one, word two, and so on. Later that day or the following day, ask the children to tell you some of these words. Do some children get them mixed up? Do some pronounce them wrongly?

Remind them that it is unkind and hurtful to make fun of someone who has speech difficulties.

Speech impairment – older children

Talk about people who have difficulty with speaking; especially people who can't say the words correctly. How do they think that children would feel if they had this problem? Ask them to give you 'feelings' words to describe how they think a child would feel. Write these on the board. Remind them that they are trying to find ways of making sure that children feel included in their school and ask them what they could do to help a child with a speech impairment to feel happy, secure and included in their class.

Write it

Ask them to choose four words from the list of feelings on the board and alongside each to write a sentence about how they would help a child who felt like this to feel included. Come together as a class and talk about what the children have written. Ask them to choose the best things to say and do if children have a speech problem.

Learning to speak

Children learn to speak gradually from birth; most speak well by the time they are three or four years old. They learn to speak by hearing the sounds of speech all around them. People who are born deaf have never heard the sounds of speech and so have to learn to speak another way, usually through mimicking the facial movements and by feeling the vocal cords vibrate in the throat. Because of this, children with hearing loss may speak indistinctly and it can be difficult to understand some of the words they say.

What could you do?

Discuss with the children how they would react to someone who speaks differently. Ask them to work in pairs and write down the kinds of things they could say and do to make someone feel at ease about speaking especially when their voice is difficult to understand.

Give them time to say what they want to say.

Don't finish their sentences for them.

Listen to them carefully.

Include children with speech impairment

Remind the children that it would be easy to exclude children who have difficulty in speaking. In a busy classroom, children may be impatient and not want to bother going to the trouble of listening.

Help them to understand that in a truly inclusive world people would want to wait and listen carefully to make sure that they understand people who have speech difficulties.

Stammer – younger children

Circle Time

Sensitivity warning. Amend the activities if a child in your class stammers.

Remind the children about the last session when you talked about children who had a speech problem. Talk about children who stammer and explain that this is an emotional problem and that someone who stammers may grow out of it or it may carry on into adult life. Ask the children if they know anyone who stammers. Sometimes people make fun of stammering people or think it is funny to pretend to stammer. Help the children to understand that this is not funny and can hurt the feelings of the person who stammers.

How would you feel?

Ask the children to think how they would feel if they could not talk easily and had a stammer and to finish the sentence: 'If I had a stammer, I would feel...' Make a list of what the children say and discuss each one.

What makes people stammer?

Explain that some people have difficulty with certain sounds. They can say all other words quite easily but when words begin with these certain sounds they just can't get these words out of their mouth. Sometimes they substitute other words that don't start with the difficult sound.

We would feel...

sad, unhappy, an outcast, no one will listen, awful, worried, can't talk, face goes red, embarrassed, self-concious.

How can you help them?

Ask the children what they could do to help someone who had a stammer. Write a list of what they say. Will all these things work? Which is the best? Ask the children to tell you if they have known a person who had a stammer and can tell you how that person managed to deal with the problem.

How can you include them?

Remind the children that it's all about thinking of the other person's feelings and putting yourself in their shoes. If they listen carefully to the person who stammers and give them time to finish their own sentences that will make the stammering person feel better. It's really important to help a person who stammers to feel good about other things they can do and not to talk about the fact that they stammer.

Stammer – older children

Sensitivity warning. Amend the activities if a child in your class stammers.

Introduce this work by talking about the words 'stammer' and 'stutter'. Stutter sounds like the sound it makes (onomatopoeia). Both words mean almost the same, although stuttering people usually involuntarily repeat the first syllables of a word whereas a stammerer may have halting altercation with pauses as well. Explain that thousands of young children stammer and most outgrow the condition. (It is said that boys are three times more likely to stammer than girls. It is estimated that as many as one percent of adults stammer and that it affects 450,000 people in the UK.)

Debate

> 'I feel really bad when people stammer and they can't get the words out. There's nothing you can do.'

Take notes of what the children say and how many think that there is nothing that we can do. Remind them of the ways they said they could help the person with a speech impairment in the previous work. Will these things also help a person who stammers?

What you can do

People who stammer function best in a calm and relaxed atmosphere, so keep calm and don't look anxious if your friend stutters. Follow this advice:

- Show you are interested in what he is saying, not how he says it.
- Look at him when he talks and then he knows you are listening and won't rush.
- Keep eye contact and don't look away when he stammers.
- Don't finish his sentence even if you know what he is trying to say.

Comedy

There are people who use stammering as part of a comedy act. Explain to children that while this often seems funny to watch on TV it really isn't funny to someone who has a stammer. Remind the children that if we are trying to make people feel included, making fun of people who have a stammer won't help.

How they feel

A child who stammers has written this about his stammering.

> 'This is what happens when the stammer comes – I get a block in my throat and my lips go all tight too – this is the stammer laughing at me.'

Discuss this statement and the effect it will have on a child who stammers. Is he going to be able to take part in discussions? How is he going to cope with people who are unkind or impatient with him?

Foreign accents — younger children

Circle Time

Ask children who have been on foreign holidays to say what it's like when they hear people in that country talking in the street. Do they like to hear foreign languages spoken or does it make them feel bad because they can't understand what the people are saying? Ask them to finish the sentence: 'When I hear someone talking in a language I can't understand, I feel...'

Talk about the many people in this country who speak their first language when they are out and about and why, even when they speak English well, they still like to use their own language with their family. Why do they think this is?

How would it feel?

Ask the children to think how it would feel for the foreign person to be in this country. Would they have the same feelings if they couldn't understand the English language? Ask them to finish the sentence: 'I think people who couldn't understand English would feel...'

Tell a story

Latifa was six years old when she came to England from Afghanistan; she couldn't speak much English then. She went to an infant school near her home and felt very unhappy in the classroom with so many children who all seemed to know everyone and everything. The teacher was very kind and found her a friend, Amy, to look after her. Amy was kind and helped her to fit in to school and helped her with words. After a very short time Latifa could speak a lot of English words and felt comfortable at school. There was only one problem. Benny was unkind, especially in the playground. He kept on mocking the way she spoke English with an accent and echoing the words she used.

Talk with the children about how Latifa would feel when Benny was being unkind. Ask them to tell you what they would like to say to Benny.

Draw and write

Ask the children to think about what they could do to help someone with a foreign accent to feel good about coming to your school. Ask them to draw a picture of themselves with the person and to write what they could do to make the person feel included.

This is me playing with Latifa. I could help her and be her friend. I would listen to what she says and help her learn new words.

Foreign accents – older children

Talk with the children about films they have seen where someone has a foreign accent. Does this make the person seem mysterious or exotic? Does the accent lend charm to the film? Can the children give examples of accents that seem exciting and glamorous?

Learning a different language

Talk about accents and how it is difficult for people to speak as a native of the country of the language they are learning. Explain that our mouths have learned to speak our mother tongue by watching faces and hearing it spoken from birth and that it can be very difficult to make the sounds of a second language. If people want to speak as a native of a country they usually have to live there for some time to immerse themselves in the culture.

Accents in our schools

More than 300 languages are spoken by children in London's schools, making the capital the most linguistically diverse city in the world. (See Information sheet at end of unit.)

Explain that while many children born in the UK whose families came from other countries speak English without any accent, there are other children who are recently in the UK from their own country who are still learning to speak English. Sometimes children with accents find it difficult to speak in a way that is readily understood by other UK children.

How can you help?

Ask the children to work in pairs and discuss how they could help a child with an accent that is hard to understand to feel included in your school. Ask them to write a numbered list. Share these ideas with the class and agree a list that can be displayed in your classroom.

1. Listen carefully to their voice.

2. Make sure you understand what they mean.

3. Help them with difficult words.

4. Make sure they are are included in class discussions.

5. Include them in your friendship group.

6. Don't treat them differently to anyone else.

7. Never criticise or make fun of their accent.

Be interested in other languages.

Ask the children to find out some words in every day use in other languages; if possible ask children from other cultures to tell you useful words from their language and encourage the children in your class to learn to pronounce these properly.

Ask children to find out what the International Phonetic Alphabet (IPA) is. Can they write their name or another word using IPA?

Regional accents — younger children

Circle Time

Explain that the English spoken in the UK has developed over many centuries, includes words from other countries and is still growing and changing. Children in various areas of the UK have different regional accents.

Our regional accent and the words we use

Discuss with the children the words they use and the accent in your area of the country. Do they know some words that are only used in your area? Is there a language underneath the accepted one in your area, such as the Cockney Rhyming slang? Can you tell the children any words that your family uses or that you know that are not generally used in your region?

A slade is a slope that runs down to the beach from the promenade in Blackpool.

New accents

If you have any children from other regions of the UK ask them to talk about how they felt when they came to your region. Could they understand what was said? Did they have to ask people to repeat what they said? Did they feel different from other children because they spoke in a different way? Did they feel excluded because of this?

Tell a story

Avery is seven and is a new boy at his school. He has moved from a different part of the UK and the accent there is very different from his new area. Some children can't really understand what he says sometimes and this makes Avery mad. They keep saying, 'What?' and he gets fed up saying things over and over again to make them understand. Sometimes he can't be bothered to say things again and just shrugs. He is finding it hard to fit in. No one seems to want to help.

Ask the children to think of Avery's feelings and the feelings of the other children in the class. Ask volunteers to answer these questions:
- What would you say to Avery?
- What would you say to Avery's teacher?
- What would you say to the other children in the class?

Draw and write

Ask the children to think of a good ending to Avery's story and to draw a picture of it. Help them to write about their ending. Discuss the various endings with the class.

Words, Words, Words Activity Sheet 1

Help the children to keep a record of new words by using this activity sheet.

Regional accents — older children

Talk to the children about the many regional accents in the UK. Centuries ago the language in these areas developed in isolation and incorporated accents of people who moved into the UK. There are not only different pronunciations of words, but in some cases different words altogether are used for the same things, for example, in Lancashire a clothes horse is called a 'maiden' and in Yorkshire a narrow passageway between houses is called a 'snicket'.

In more recent times BBC Standard English or Received Pronunciation (RP) developed in London and nearby counties was, at first, the only accent heard on the radio and TV. If the children watch really old TV programmes they will be able to hear this accent but today very few people use it apart from the royal family. Nowadays people think RP is a 'posh' accent and are keen to protect and preserve regional accents.

What accents do you know?

Ask the children to say what they know of other regional accents. Can some of them speak using other accents? Mimics in your class will probably be able to speak like people they hear on TV or in films. Remind them that though this may be a bit of fun, mimicking the accent of a child in your class is hurtful and can be seen as a kind of verbal bullying.

How do you sound?

When we visit other regions in this country and are surprised at their regional accents, do we realise that our accents sound strange to their ears? Talk about the ability that some people have of tuning in to accents when they are visiting other parts of the country and how these people find they are speaking in a similar way.

Be sensitive

Having explored various accents, help the children to understand that people from other regions are often very proud of their dialect and may not want to change it to the one where you live. Remind the children that the way we speak is part of our personality and that it can be very hurtful to joke about or ridicule anyone's accent.

Inclusion

If children come to your school from other regions, the children in your class may not be able to understand their dialect very well at first until their ears become used to the sound. Ask the children to think of ways they can make children with regional accents feel comfortable in your class or school. Ask them what kinds of things they can do to make sure these children do not feel excluded at first.

Words, Words, Words Activity Sheet 2

Ask the children to complete this and discuss some of the interesting words they write.

Words, Words, Words Activity Sheet 1

Ask the children to keep this activity sheet for a whole week and list any new words they come across in their reading or talking.

New word	Meaning

Turn over the paper. Write sentences using two of these new words.

Words, Words, Words Activity Sheet 2

Ask the children to use dictionaries, the internet and their families to find out new and interesting words. Can they write down the origin or region where the word came from and its meaning.

New word or phrase	Origin or region	What it means

Turn over the paper. Compose and write down sentences using some of these words.

Information sheet

20 most common languages in London schools, 2006

Research has revealed that more than 300 languages are spoken by children in London's schools, making the capital the most linguistically diverse city in the world. Although English remains overwhelmingly the most common first language, for more than a third of children it is not the language they will speak or hear spoken at home.

Language	Approximate total
English	608, 500
Bengali and Sylheti	40,400
Punjabi	29,800
Gujarati	28,600
Hindu/Urdu	26,000
Turkish	15,600
Arabic	11,000
English – based Creoles	10,700
Yoruba (Nigeria)	10,400
Somali	8,300
Cantonese	6,900
Greek	6,300
Akan (Ashanti)	6,000
Portuguese	6,000
French	5,600
Spanish	5,500
Tamil (Sri Lanka, Tamil Nadu – India)	3,700
Farsi (Persian)	3,300
Italian	2,500
Vietnamese	2,400

from: http://www.literacytrust.org.uk/Database/stats/EALstats.html#20languages

Unit 5

Information sheet

Other languages

Before 1000 BC

Sumerian – c. 3450 BC: Ideographic tablets from the temple archives in Uruk

Egyptian – c. 3320 BC: A collection of labels from tomb Uj, perhaps belonging to King Scorpion, in the Umm el-Qa'ab[3][2]

Eblaite – c. 2400 BC

Akkadian – c. 2300 BC

Elamite – c. 2250 BC: Awan dynasty peace treaty with Naram-Sin

West Semitic / proto-Canaanite – c. 1800 BC: Middle Bronze Age alphabets

Luwian – c. 1800 BC

Hittite – c. 1650 BC: Various cuneiform texts and Palace Chronicles written during the reign of Hattusili I, from the archives at Hattusas

Minoan – c. 1600 BC: Linear A

Canaanite – c. 1500 BC: Proto-Canaanite alphabet

Greek – c. 1450 BC

Chinese – c. 1300 BC: Oracle bone script[4]

Ugaritic – c. 1300 BC

http://en.wikipedia.org/wiki/List_of_languages_by_first_written_accounts#Before_1000_BC

Programming language

A programming language is an artificial language that can be used to control the behavior of a machine, particularly a computer. Programming languages, like human languages, are defined through the use of syntactic and semantic rules, to determine structure and meaning respectively.

Programming languages are used to facilitate communication about the task of organising and manipulating information, and to express algorithms precisely. Some authors restrict the term 'programming language' to those languages that can express all possible algorithms; sometimes the term 'computer language' is used for more limited artificial languages.

From: http://en.wikipedia.org/wiki/Language#Formal_languages

5

Extension activities for younger children

Research

Ask each child to find out the meaning of these surnames:
- Cooper
- Smith
- Johnson
- Beckham
- Potter.

This website will help. http://surnames.behindthename.com/

Ask them to find the meaning of their own surname. They can ask their family or use books. Some meanings of surnames are difficult to find.

Take home record sheet

Ask the children to make a record of one thing that they have learned during this unit that they didn't know before. Ask them to illustrate this record and to take it home to share with their family.

Investigation

Ask the children to listen to part of the video on Anna on this website. Anna is a deaf child who is learning to speak: http://www.oraldeafed.org/movies/index.html

Ask the children if watching this clip has made them more aware of the difficulties of children with speech difficulties.

Ask them to write about Anna.

Rhyming slang

Do the children know about rhyming slang? Explain what this is and give them some examples. The following website will help: http://www.cockneyrhymingslang.co.uk/slang/apples_and_pears

Ask the children to work in pairs to make up some rhyming slang examples of their own. Share these.

Poster

Ask the children to design a poster to make people more aware of the importance of speech and language. Choose a slogan such as 'Listen to us' or 'It's good to talk' and encourage the children to use all media to illustrate their poster.

Silent game

Divide the class into pairs. Gather one from each pair and tell them to make their partner do something without using words, for example, sit down, jump three times or move to a certain part of the room. You could say that the one who does it is the winner. Change over.

Extension activities for older children

Research

Ask the children to work in pairs and to visit this website to see pictures and writing done by children who have a stammer: http://www.stammertrust.co.uk/pdf/drawings.pdf

Ask the children to make notes of what the children who stammer say about how stammering makes them feel. When all the children have visited the website discuss what they have seen and how they now feel about people who stammer. Ask them if visiting this website has made them more aware of the feelings of people who stammer and if they now know how to help people who stammer.

Take home record sheet

Write a list of all the parts in this unit on the board. Ask the children to use these as headings and to write a brief description of what they have learned from doing the work. Ask them to take their list home to share with their family.

Investigation 1

http://www.collectbritain.co.uk/collections/dialects/

This website has clips of different accents. As a class, listen to one clip and ask the children to jot down any words they don't know. Talk about the accent; explain words they jotted down. Repeat this using a different clip. Ask the children to use the Words, Words, Words Activity Sheet 2 to make a glossary of new words and phrases. There are notes on the website to help teachers about various words or sentence construction.

Investigation 2

Use this website to find out about languages in the world.

http://www.vistawide.com/languages/language_statistics.htm

Ask the children to work in pairs and find out one important or interesting fact about languages in the world. Ask them to write down this fact and share it with the rest of the class. Make a final list, excluding any duplicates and read through the information. Discuss what the children have learned and how they now feel at speaking their own language.

Can you tell?

There are a lot of foreign language stations on TV and the radio. Ask the children to listen to some of these at home and try to tell from the sound what the language is. Ask them to give themselves a score out of ten. Discuss this in Circle Time.

Spellings

Remind the children about the vagaries of spelling in the English language. Ask them to choose a few words they know and write the words as they sound alongside the correct spelling. Discuss why some English words have strange spellings.

Reflect and remember

This unit has been about helping children to understand that many people speak differently for various reasons. Some children may feel excluded because of this and we must help them to recognise the importance of listening carefully to what people say and accepting them into their group even if they do speak differently.

At the end of this unit talk about all the things the children have learned. Remind them that you have all been learning about people who speak differently, whether they have a speech impairment, stammer, foreign accent or different UK dialect and making sure that they all feel included, especially when they speak differently from most people in the class. They have been learning about the feelings of people who stammer and the things they can do to help someone who has this condition.

Circle Time

Ask the children to think about one thing that they have learned and to finish the sentence: 'I have learned that...'

Ask them if they now feel empathy towards people who have a different kind of speech from them and ask them to finish the sentence: 'I know that people who speak differently from the rest of the class may feel...'

Outside school

Remind the children that accepting people and relating to them doesn't stop at the classroom door. They will meet many people outside school who speak differently and they must make sure that people who speak differently never feel excluded.

It could be you

Remind the children that they themselves may move to a different country or region of this country and that they will then be the one with a different kind of speech.

We really want all children to understand, feel empathy for and include children with speech problems or different accents, whether from this country or from a different country.

Unit 6. Gender roles and stereotypes

We want all children to understand, feel empathy for and include all children whether they are male or female. There should be no, 'You can't play because you're a boy,' comments, or remarks such as, 'She's only a girl,' in our schools. We want all children to feel that they are valued whatever their gender and to know that they can take on any role whether a long ago traditional male or female one.

In this unit there are activities under these headings:

- Old and traditional gender roles

- Male and female roles

- Toys

- Stories and books

- Games

- Media and advertising.

This unit is concerned with how we and children act towards those of the opposite gender. It also has activities concerned with gender expectations and types of sterotyping.

Websites

The role of men, women and children in ancient Greece:

http://oncampus.richmond.edu/academics/education/projects/webunits/greecerome/Greeceroles1.html

Education in colonial days:

http://www.stratfordhall.org/ed-boysgirls.html

An article relating to gender specific toys:

http://findarticles.com/p/articles/mi_m2294/is_9-10_53/ai_n16084036

An article about children and gender stereotypes:

http://www.media-awareness.ca/english/resources/tip_sheets/gender_tip.cfm

6

Old and traditional gender roles – younger children

Circle Time

Talk to the children about the traditional, old fashioned gender roles and the ways that the family was organised in the olden days. Do they have stories about the people in their family where only the male parent went to work and the female parent stayed at home and looked after the home and family? Ask the children to think why this was and to finish the sentence: 'In the olden days the mother stayed at home because...' Make a list of their responses on the board.

In the olden days, Mother stayed home to do the washing.

Draw and write

Ask the children to choose a mother's work as listed on the board and to draw the mother in the home. Ask them to write a sentence about it. Display the children's work under a heading such as 'In the olden days...'

Ask the children to think of the traditional male parent's role in the olden days, when he was in sole charge of work and money as the only breadwinner when the mother stayed at home to look after him and the family. Mothers were often seen as not good enough to do many things. Was this true?

Large families

Talk to the children about the large families that our ancestors had and the need for the young children to go to work as soon as they were old enough. Do they know that very young children had to leave school at age ten or eleven and go to work? Discuss what your children think about that.

Some working wives

Explain that in the early 20th Century women were needed in mills and factories and some of these works offered a 'housewives shift' in the evening so that the father could be at home to be with children while the mother worked.

Remind them that not many women of rich families ever worked at all. They stayed at home with their parents until they married and had their own home. They were excluded from having a career. Was this fair?

Old and traditional gender roles – older children

Talk to the children about the ideas on the facing page before having a discussion about the old roles of men and women. Explain that in the past:

- many girls from rich families were educated at home instead of school
- many young boys from rich families were sent away to boarding school
- children rarely left home until they were married
- some boys and men went to universities but women were never allowed to go
- women were not allowed to vote in elections
- most careers or well paid jobs were for men
- most women who worked were in very low paid jobs
- until the 1960s men were paid more than women for doing the same work.

Discussion

Explain that gender roles were very carefully defined in the olden days. Ask them why they think this was. Discuss each response offered.

Ask the children to think what caused changes in the old traditional roles of people and discuss these, for example, smaller families, household appliances, more opportunities.

Do the children know of countries where even today the old and traditional roles of men and women are still in place, where girls and women are seen as inferior and excluded from having money or taking decisions about their families?

In other countries

Ask the children to work together to find out about the traditional roles of men and women from one other country. They could use websites such as the one about ancient Greece.

Education

Explain that education was traditionally for boys while girls were not thought to need educating; their role, whether rich or poor was to be a mother in charge of the house. It was thought that women were not clever enough to have a career and for many years they were not allowed to have a good education or a career. They were not included.

Work at home

Ask the children to talk with their families, particularly grandparents, about the gender roles that were in place when they were children. Ask them to make a list of the differences between then and now and to bring this to school for discussion.

6

Male and female roles – younger children

Circle Time

If necessary explain the words 'male' and 'female'. Talk with the children about the present day roles of parents or carers and the children. Do all their male carers go to work or do some stay at home to look after the children? Do all female carers stay at home or do some go to work? Ask volunteers to say who looks after them at home by finishing this sentence: 'At my home, my...'

At my home, my auntie cares for me after school, Mum looks after me before school and Dad puts me to bed and reads to me at night.

Four draw and write activities

The purpose of these is to elicit from the children the gender of the person doing the job. You may wish to add others more applicable in your area.

1. Ask the children to draw a doctor helping a child who is ill.
   Ask them to write the name of the doctor and what they are doing.

2. Ask the children to draw a nurse helping a sick man.
   Ask them to write the name of the nurse and what they are doing.

3. Ask the children to draw someone delivering the post at their house.
   Ask them to write the name of this person and what they are doing.

4. Ask the children to draw a person cutting down a tree.
   Ask them to write the name of this person and what they are doing.

Note down how many children have chosen to draw males or females doing these jobs. Talk about why the children have chosen that gender. Do they see particular jobs as for men or for women? If so how can we change this to make it more inclusive?

Jobs for the boys/girls

Ask the boys to tell you the job they would like to have when they are grown up. Make a list of these.

Ask the girls to tell you the job they would like to do and make a second list. Are some jobs on both lists?

Do your young children see some jobs as particularly male jobs or female jobs? Talk to the boys about their reasons for choosing their job and whether they think the girls could do it. Talk about the girl's choice of jobs and whether boys could do them.

Talk about the following statement:

Is it fair to exclude people from doing the job they want to do because of their gender?

Male and female roles — older children

Debate

Which of these statements is true?

1. Nowadays it doesn't much matter what gender you are; if you want to do something, whether it is sport, work or study, there are opportunities for all.

2. There is still gender discrimination. Some girls and women can't do some sports or have some occupations, neither can men.

After the debate, ask the children to vote on which they think is the truest statement.

Sport

Make a list of sports. Talk about whether it is possible for either gender to do any of these sports or whether some are seen as for men only or for women only. Why is this?

Clothing

Talk about why it is accepted for girls and women to wear clothing that looks manly, for example, tailored suits, and not acceptable for men and boys to wear clothing that women and girls normally wear, for example, skirts, frilly dresses, flamboyant hats.

Debate

Women and girls are the weaker sex.

After the debate, count how many children agree and how many disagree with this statement. Ask those who think it is true to explain the reasons for thinking this.

Running a home

Discuss the following:

Do parents or carers have equal responsibility in the running of the home? What are the modern day roles in their home? How do people organise the sharing out of responsibilities? Can the woman choose to clean the car and mow the lawn? What if the man doesn't want to do the cooking and clean the house?

Ask the children to give examples of the kinds of sharing of responsibilities in homes they know about.

Who is the breadwinner?

Now that there is more gender equality it can happen that women earn more money and have higher prestige jobs than men. Talk about whether this can make difficulties in life outside work.

Work at home

Are some people still excluded from joining groups or clubs because of their gender? Ask the children to find examples of places where women or men are not allowed to participate.

6

Toys – younger children

Circle Time

Talk about baby toys. Can any of the children tell you of the toy they liked best when they were a toddler? Ask them to finish the sentence: 'When I was a toddler my best toy was...'

When I was a toddler my best toy was my teddy.

Talk with the children about the toys they like to play with now. Ask them to finish the sentence, 'The toy I like best is...' Make a list of all the toys mentioned. Read through your lists and ask the children if they think there are some toys that are more suitable for boys and some more for girls. Draw different coloured rings around these words. Ask the children why they think some toys are gender specific.

Which don't you have?

Ask the children to look at the list of toys and to think of one toy on the list that they would like that they don't have. Find out which toys the girls would like to have and draw a different coloured ring around these. Does this tell you anything about toys and gender?

Do the same for the boys. Does this tell you anything about toys and gender?

Classroom toys

Talk about toys in the classroom. Ask the children to think of two toys there that they like the best. Ask them to draw each of these toys on a piece of paper and to write the name of the toys and why they like them. Come together as a group and write up the names of the toys they chose. Count how many girls and boys chose each toy. Make a class chart of these findings using a picture of each toy alongside the numbers of girls and boys who like it. Display this with some speech bubbles such as: 'Which toy do boys like best? Which do girls like best? Which toy is liked by most boys and girls?' Ask yourself whether this small survey tells you something about the toys you provide for children in the classroom. Do you need more non- gender specific toys?

Work at home

Ask the children to take a good look at their toys at home and to make a list of how many animal toys they have, how many toys in the shape of people or teddies they have and how many vehicle toys they have. Collate this data for boys and girls. Discuss any interesting findings. Talk about whether there should be toys specifically for boys or girls.

Toys Activity Sheet 1

Ask the children to complete this activity sheet. Talk about what they have drawn and written.

Toys — older children

Debate

Debate these two statements:

> 1. 'Some toys are designed specifically for boys and some for girls.'
> 2. 'Toys are designed for children irrespective of whether they are boys or girls.'

Ask the children to vote on which statement they think is correct. Why?

1977 survey

A survey in 1977 looking at toys for children aged 1-6 found that while children mainly had the same number of books, musical items and stuffed animals, boys had a greater variety of toys, and tended to have more toys overall. There were also differences in the kinds of toys that boys and girls possessed. Boys had more vehicles (e.g. toy cars and trucks) with 375 vehicles in the boys' rooms and 17 in the girls. Boys had more 'spatial-temporal' toys (e.g. shape-sorting toys, clocks, magnets, outer-space toys); they also had more sports equipment (e.g. balls, skates, kites), toy animals, garages or depots, machines, military toys and educational and art materials (despite the fact that these may be seen as gender-neutral). (See website http://findarticles.com/p/articles/mi_m2294/is_9-10_53/ai_n16084036 for more details.) Ask the children in your class to think whether their toys at home are specifically for their gender. Ask them to write a list of the five toys they like the best and to write alongside these whether they are gender neutral. Share these lists.

What do the lists tell us?

Talk about whether boys would like some of the toys the girls put on their list and whether girls would like some of the boys' chosen toys. Do these toys show gender stereotyping? Discuss whether the choice of toys influence the roles that children take on in society.

Toys Activity Sheet 2

Ask the children to complete the activity sheet. Or ask them to write their feelings about the toys they have at home. Do their own toys show gender stereotyping?

Design a toy

Ask the children to work in pairs and design a toy that would appeal to boys and girls alike. Ask them to draw this toy, describe its appearance and to write how both boys and girls would play with it.

Do toys prolong the myth that boys are different from girls?

Discuss whether a girl in a family of all girls is restricted by not having toys often thought of as for boys and vice versa. Do toys widen the gender gap? How important is it for parents and others to make sure that there are gender neutral toys for their children? Will this help in making sure that people are more gender inclusive?

6

Stories and books – younger children

Circle Time

Ask the children to think of the male and female characters in some of the stories you have told them recently. Choose one story and ask how the story would have been different if the main character had been of the opposite gender. Would the outcome have been the same? Can the children suggest a different outcome to the story with gender reversal?

Talk about the roles of people in some of the stories that you have told them recently. Have all the females had traditional female roles to play? Have some of them played traditional roles of the opposite gender. Talk about why some stories could reinforce the old fashioned stereotypical gender roles.

Tell a story

Tell the children the story of Cinderella. Ask them to think of the role of Cinderella, her sisters and the prince. Now ask the children to think about the same story where Cinderella was a boy called Cinderbert. How would this story change? Ask them to finish the sentence; 'If Cinderella had been a boy...'

> If Cinderella had been Cinderbert, he might not have had to do the housework. He might have had a fairy godfather to help him.

New Story People Activity Sheet 1

Talk the children through the activity sheet and ask them to complete it. Share their work and talk about the different roles they have portrayed.

Classroom books

Ask the children to think of the books they used when learning to read and the books in the class library. Do these books reinforce the old traditional male female roles or are they more inclusive with men and women, girls and boys taking on the roles of each other? Ask the children to tell you of stories they know that are gender inclusive and vice versa.

Have you story books that show males in roles where they are the caregiver to the family and where females are the main breadwinner? Talk about the difference between old fashioned books where this was not the case and make a short list of any stories or books that are modern gender neutral.

Write a story

Ask the children to write a story where the characters have gender neutral roles and to illustrate their story. Display these with speech bubbles about the stories such as: 'Daddy takes the children to school while Mum goes to work', or 'Mum is cleaning the car and Dad washes up before he puts the baby to bed'. Remind the children of the importance of thinking of people as people not as boys or girls.

Books Activity Sheet 1

Ask children to choose a book to draw and write about on this activity sheet.

Stories and books – older children

Discuss

Tell the children that you want them to think about the books they read and whether some books reinforce the stereotypical male female gender roles. Can they give you some examples of stories where this happens? Can they give you examples of any stories where male and female roles are gender neutral? Ask them to think of this when they are reading.

Debate

Ask the children which of the following statements is the truest and why.

'In most stories the stereotypical gender roles of male and female are reinforced.'
'In most stories the inclusive or neutral roles of male and female are reinforced.'

Early reading

Ask the children to think back to their earliest memories of reading and learning to read. Did some of these learning to read books reinforce the stereotypically male and female roles? Ask them to give some examples.

New Story People Activity Sheet 2

Ask the children to complete this activity sheet. Remind them that a nursery rhyme actually has to rhyme.

Books Activity Sheet 2

Ask the children, working in pairs, to select a book they know well from your class library. Ask them to write a report on the gender specifics of that book, to list any examples of gender stereotyping as well as gender neutral behaviour in the book.

Then ask them to work alone, choose a different book and complete the activity sheet.

Change a story

Ask the children to select a traditional nursery story that is well known. Change the gender of the main characters, alter the story to make sure it is gender neutral and illustrate the story. Display the stories under a heading such as 'Gender neutral children's stories'.

Write a story

It has been said that picture books provide prolonged and repeated exposure to parenting techniques and related gender roles. Ask the children to write a story for young children about a child, animal or creature. Make the parenting of the character in the story gender neutral. Is it hard to do this? Discuss whether such stories will help children to be more inclusive.

Ensure the children realise they have a role to play in promoting gender inclusion.

6

Games — younger children

Circle Time

Talk with the children about the games they play in the playground. Ask the children to tell you the playground game they like the best by finishing the sentence: 'The playground game I like best is...' Make a list of these games on the board.

Ask the children whether they think that some playground games on the list are more for boys or more for girls or whether they are for boys and girls. Using the list you have made, draw a ring around those that they think are for all children regardless of gender. Talk about this. What about the other games; are they really gender specific?

Games outside school

Ask the children to think of the games they play out of school. They can be board games, family games or physical games. Ask them to think of one game they like to play that girls and boys can join in. Ask them to draw a picture of themselves playing this gender neutral game, to name the game and write why they like it.

This is me playing cricket on the beach. I like it because all my family join in.

Grown up games

Ask the children to help you to make a list of grown up games and sports, such as football, tennis and cricket, hockey, sailing, polo. Discuss whether mainly men play these games, whether mainly women and whether all games are suitable for both men and women. Talk about whether there are men's teams and women's teams or whether both genders can play together as equals. Are there different rules for when men and women play? Are there sometimes mixed teams? Talk about the different physical attributes of men and women and why there sometimes have to be differences in how people play. Read the list you made. Use colour to indicate which are mainly for males, females or gender neutral.

Games We Play Activity Sheet 1

Ask the children to help you to make a list of games that children play and write these up under two headings: Indoor games, outdoor games. Ask the children to use these lists to help them to complete the activity sheet.

Read this scenario

Glen was popular with boys in his class because he was good at games. Every playtime in summer he would play cricket with his friends. These friends were all boys. One day a girl called Sharina asked if she could play. Glen said she couldn't play because she was a girl.

- Ask the children what they think of Glen for saying that.
- What would they have said to him if they had been there?
- What could Sharina do?

Was Glen being a good includer? Ask the children if they would ever exclude a girl or boy from their game.

Games – older children

Indoor and outdoor games

Talk about the kinds of games that the children like to play indoors and make a list of these. Are these games on the list equally suitable for girls and boys? Write down any conclusions from the discussion. Do the same activity with outdoor games and discuss any differences.

Inclusion or exclusion

Talk with the children of their responses to the different games above. Is it easier to include both genders in indoor games or outdoor games? Why do they think this is?

Electronic games discussion

Discuss the depiction of characters in electronic games. Ask the children to describe the physical characteristics of males and females depicted in these games. Are all the females beautiful and weak? Are the males strong and heavily built? Are there games where the female heroines are ugly and strong; male heroes ugly and weak?

Are some electronic games designed for boys and some for girls? Are the characters in these games depicted differently? Are the 'baddies' always ugly? Do the boys do macho things and are girls too much concerned with their appearance and beauty?

Games We Play Activity Sheet 2

Discuss the differences between indoor games, informal games and sports and come to an agreement about what these terms mean to you. Ask the children to complete this activity sheet. Collect their papers and talk about the games they have drawn and written about and whether they are for boys, girls or are gender neutral.

Debate

Ask children to work in pairs to write a list of arguments for and against the following statement:

> 'Males are better at some games than others and so are females.'

Come together as a group and argue this out. What conclusion do the children come to? Can they come to a consensus? Can they write a better statement that is more inclusive?

Inclusion or exclusion

Ask the children to think carefully about excluding people from games or activities. Remind them that people are people first and that there should be no difference because of gender.

6

Media and advertising – younger children

Circle Time

Talk with the children about people they see on children's TV. Are all the girl children unreal, beautiful and clever or do some of them look like children you see in the streets?

Ask the children to tell you which characters look unreal and are a stereotype. Ask them to help you to make a list of all the stereotypical characters they know on children's TV.

How does it make you feel?

Talk about how ordinary children feel when they see super girls and boys on children's TV. Does it make them feel they are not good enough? Does it make them feel they want to try to be different? Ask them to finish the sentence: 'When I watch super heroes on TV it makes me feel... about myself.' Make two lists of the words they use under 'good feelings' and 'bad feelings'. Which is the longer list?

Ordinary girls and boys

Ask the children to think of advertising on TV where children are represented. Can they think of advertisements where the children look glamorous and unreal? Write these down. Can they think of adverts where children look normal and everyday? Write these down. Discuss the adverts in both lists. Do they think that children have been chosen for the adverts because they are really good looking or handsome? Is this a good idea?

Tell a story

> Karl was seven years old and was not very tall, not very thin, not very strong and not very good looking. When he looked in a mirror he was sad about how he looked. He knew that his mum loved him because she said so but he didn't really love himself. He watched children's TV after school and when he saw the handsome children in some of the programmes it made him feel even worse about himself.

Ask the children to think about the story and answer the questions:

- What would you like to say to Karl?
- What could you do to make Karl feel better about himself?
- How could you make sure that Karl felt included in school?

Write the ending

Tell or write a good ending to Karl's story where you help him to do something that helps him to feel included at school. Draw a picture about your ending.

Media and advertising – older children

General discussion

Talk to the children about the way young and old people are depicted on TV. Explain that many of the roles show people as stereotypes with girls and young women interested only in themselves, beauty and appearance; men and boys depicted as macho beings. Explain that the ways people are depicted can have a long lasting effect on people who watch the programmes, especially if they are not able to see that these are stereotypes and not real people. Discuss the portrayal of people of different nationalities, religions, ages and backgrounds. Discuss the portrayal of rich people from wealthy backgrounds as well as poor people.

Children's TV

Give the children opportunities to discuss the portrayal of young girls and boys on children's TV programmes. Can they think of programmes that depict children in a realistic way? Talk about these characters and programmes. Can they think of programmes that depict children in a stereotypical way? Discuss these.

I like to watch Superman. He is kind, helps people and a good role-model.

Ask them to work in pairs with a child of different gender and to think of one specific programme that they both watch regularly. Ask each of them to choose one character of different gender to themselves and list behaviour and appearance which is normal and which is stereotypical. Still in their pairs, ask the children to read what their partner has written and discuss whether they agree. Come together as a group and discuss which, if any, of these characters provide good role-models for children.

Soaps

Ask the children to help you to make a list of the soaps that they watch. Ask the children to tell you of any characters' behaviours which could be thought of as excluding. Talk about why they think this. Discuss the possible outcomes of this excluding behaviour.

Magazines and comics

Talk about the appearance and behaviour of super heroes in young people's periodicals. Though these are for amusement and for fun, ask the children to discuss any portrayal which could cause children to be dissatisfied with their own appearance and behaviour.

Remind children that everyone is equal and that no one should ever feel excluded.

6

Toys Activity Sheet 1

Unit 6

My name is...

Draw the toys that boys and girls usually have.

Boys	Girls
This is...	This is...
This is...	This is...
This is...	This is...

Turn over the paper. Draw your special toy. Write about it.

Toys Activity Sheet 2

My name is..

Boys and girls seem to prefer different toys. Why?

Boys like... because	Girls like... because
Boys like... because	Girls like... because
Boys like... because	Girls like... because
Boys like... because	Girls like... because

Turn over and draw your favourite toy and write why you like it. Would someone of the opposite gender like this toy? Why?

Draw some toys that boys and girls both like. Write down why you think that both boys and girls like these.

New Story People Activity Sheet 1

My name is ....

Draw and write about these new story people.

	Write what Old Father Hubberd does at home.
This is Old Father Hubberd.	
	Write what Little Girl Blue does.
This is Little Girl Blue.	

Turn over the paper. Choose a different nursery story character and change the gender. Draw the person and write a sentence about them.

New Story People Activity Sheet 2

My name is ....

Think of two characters in stories you have recently read. Change the gender and write a little about what the new character does.

The original male character was... This is a picture of my new female character.	She...
The original female character was... This is a picture of my new male character.	He...

Turn over the paper and write a nursery rhyme about Little Bob Peep. Where does he live, what does he do? Illustrate your work.

Books Activity Sheet 1

My name is...

Write about a book you have read.

My book is called:

....

....

The author's name is:

....

It was written in the year:

....

The story is about:

....

....

....

....

I think this is a book for girls.
I think this is a book for boys.
I think this is a book for boys and girls.

Turn over the paper.
Think of another book, one that is for boys and girls. Draw a picture about the book. Write the name of the book and its author.

Unit 6

Books Activity Sheet 2

My name is...

Title:
Author:
Date of publication:
Example of gender neutral behaviour with page number. Page____
Example of gender neutral behaviour with page number. Page ____
Example of gender stereotypical behaviour with page number. Page ____
Example of gender stereotypical behaviour with page number. Page ____
How could you change one of the above examples to show gender neutral behaviour?

Write a report on the back of this paper about how gender neutral the book is overall. Give it marks out of 10, with 10 being gender neutral and 1 being gender stereotypical.

Games We Play Activity Sheet 1

My name is...

Think of two outdoor games you play and draw and write about them.

Game 1 draw here.	Write here.
Game 2 draw here.	Write here.

Are these games for boys, girls or both girls and boys? Finish the sentences.

My game 1 is for...

My game 2 is for...

Turn over the paper.
Draw an indoor game for boys and girls. Say why this game is good for both boys and girls.

Games We Play Activity Sheet 2

My name is ....

Write down the names of several games in the correct column.

Indoor games	Informal games	Sports

Choose one game from each column and describe how it is played, who usually plays it and whether it is suitable for both boys and girls or not.

Indoor game
Informal game
Sport

Turn over and write about whether each game could be said to be inclusive.

Would some rules need to be changed to make each game inclusive?

Unit 6

Extension activities for younger children

Research

Assemble pages from a toy catalogue. If you can, give one set to each group. Alternatively put the pages in a central place for each child to visit during the day.

Ask each child to:

- count the total number of toys
- count the toys that are mainly for boys
- count the toys that are gender neutral
- count the toys that are mainly for girls.

Ask the children to write down their findings and come together as a class and ask each child to tell the class their numbers. These will vary from child to child. Discuss why this is and why one child may think a toy is gender neutral, while another child will think it gender specific.

Take home record sheet

Ask the children to make a record of one thing that they have learned during this unit that they didn't know before. Ask them to illustrate this record and to take it home to share with their family.

Investigation

Ask the children to interview the other children in a group of six (or in their working group) to find out each child's favourite two toys. Ask them to write down the name of the person, their gender and the names (or pictures) of the two toys. They will have 12 toys listed and some will be duplicates. Ask the children, still in their groups, to put together all the information about all the toys and find the answers to these questions:

- How many boys in the group?
- How many toys are mainly for boys?
- How many toys altogether are gender neutral?
- How many girls in the group?
- How many are mainly for girls?

Ask the children to appoint a spokesperson then come together as a class to present their findings. Discuss these.

Discuss

'The toys that boys choose are gender exclusive; they are to do with things boys would like to do when they are grown up.'

Ask the children if they think this is true or false. At the end of the discussion ask children to vote.

Poster

Ask the children to make a poster with the voting outcome of the above discussion activity.

Pantomime dames

Ask the children to tell you what they know about pantomime dames. Are these always men? Why?

Extension activities for older children

Research

Ask the children to work in groups with fiction or non fiction books in the classroom library. Ask them to organise themselves to find out the numbers of fiction books and non fiction books. Discuss with the children why you, as teacher, chose this balance.

Ask pairs from half the class to take a random selection of ten books from the non fiction section; ask the rest to use ten books from the fiction section. Ask the pairs to write down the title and whether they think the book is gender neutral. Discuss these findings and why some children might decide differently about the gender neutrality of various books.

Take home record sheet

Write a list of all the parts of this unit on the board. Ask the children to use these as headings and to write a brief description of what they have learned from doing the work. Ask them to take their list home to share with their family.

Investigation 1

Ask each child to write down the title and author of every one of the books he owns at home and to write alongside whether each book is gender specific or gender neutral. Ask the children to work in groups in the classroom and put the numerical data together under the three headings; gender neutral, mainly for boys, mainly for girls. Ask each group to present their work as a chart and to display it for everyone to see. Discuss these presentations.

Investigation 2

Ask children to work at home and collect adverts from magazines. Ask them to bring these to school and put them in two separate piles, one showing traditional roles of males and females and one showing non-traditional roles. Discuss as a class the choices and whether each advert has been put in the correct pile.

Investigation 3

Ask the children to find out at home why men took female roles in Shakespearean times and why pantomime dames are always men. Discuss their findings in class.

Poster

Ask each child to choose one toy, book or game and to make a poster on A4 paper advertising this. Ask them to include on the poster whether it is for boys, girls or gender neutral.

Discuss

'The toys that children are given to play with will influence the roles that they will later take on in society.'

After the discussion, ask children to vote on whether they think this statement is true or false.

6

Reflect and remember

This unit has been concerned with how we and children act towards those of the opposite gender and how some children could feel bad about themselves or excluded because of this.

We have worked towards helping children to understand, feel empathy for and include all children whether they are male or female so that all children feel that they are valued whatever their gender and know that they can take on any role whether a traditional male or female one.

Circle Time

Ask the children to look at any displayed work and to think what they have learned from the activities and discussion in this unit and to finish the sentence:

'I have learned...'

Outside school

Remind children that when they are grown up they have as much right as someone of the opposite gender to do any sport, play games or work at any occupation.

It could be you

Remind the children that they have to look carefully at books, games, TV and advertising to watch out for and identify stereotypes so that they do not fall in to the trap of looking at or judging people through stereotyping eyes.

Remind them to make sure that they never exclude children from their group, games or friendships because they are of the opposite gender.

Unit 7. Bullying and low self-esteem

We really want all children to understand the importance of including all children in their activities and in their world whether at school or at home.

There should be no, 'You can't play because you're no good,' comments, or remarks such as, 'I'm not letting her play because she'll spoil the game.' We want all children to understand what it must feel like to be bullied, put down and made to feel not good enough to be included. We want children to know that they are valued for themselves, their personal strengths and confidence as well as for what they can offer.

> This unit is concerned with how we and children act towards others, both in and out of school. It has activities concerned with various types of bullying and how to improve low self-esteem.

In this unit there are activities about including people under the headings:

- Bullying
- Name-calling
- Threatening behaviour
- Self-esteem.

There are three paired activity sheets. The following are not tied to any particular activities and will fit in anywhere in this unit.

Included or Excluded? 1

This asks children to decide what including and excluding are and to give practical examples.

Included or Excluded? 2

This is a check sheet about whether they feel included or excluded. Instructions are on the activity sheet and you may want to cut or blank off the instructions before copying them for the children to use.

Think of a Story 1 and 2

These are about thinking of a story where someone is excluded. The children can choose any story they know.

7

Bullying – younger children

Circle Time

Ask the children what they think bullying is. Make a list of their responses. Read through the list with the children and talk about each one. Here we are thinking of the kind of exclusion that people who bully others like to create, so if they haven't offered this as a kind of bullying, talk about it now.

Friendship groups

Children sometimes think that they 'own' their friends and that these friends shouldn't have other friends. Help children to understand that it is good for them and others to have lots of different friends and different friendship groups and that within these groups there will be children who want to belong and others who don't.

I want to join in

Ask the children if there have been times when they have wanted to join in a group and were not allowed in. Ask volunteers to say how this felt. Ask children if there have been times when they have been in a game and someone else wanted to join in and they didn't want them to.

Can they give reasons why this will sometimes be OK for children not to join in immediately, for example, to make teams uneven, or right at the end of a game. Can they give reasons why this will not be OK, for example, if someone always deliberately keeps someone out from games and makes them feel bad about not being allowed in.

Draw a picture

Ask the children to draw two pictures. The first of a time when it would be OK not to let someone in a game and on the other side the second picture of a time when it would be a kind of bullying to exclude them. Ask the children to write a sentence for each picture or to explain what is happening.

Say it well

Remind the children that there are different ways of saying things; an acceptable and kind way and a horrid, unkind way. Ask them to give examples of how you could

When we've finished this game you can join in.

explain that people can't join in at present, giving an acceptable reason.

Remind the children that excluding children for no good reason is a kind of bullying.

Bullying — older children

Discuss various bullying tactics and how excluding children can be bullying. Ask the children if there are ever times when they are right in not allowing someone to join in a game or group activity. Collect their responses and list them. Go through these responses and ask all the children if they agree that these times are permissible, for example, if it is a game for two and a third person would make it impossible or if they are speaking privately about something personal. Talk about how their tone of voice and the words they use can make sure the person being kept out is not hurt or thinks they are just being horrid or unkind.

Ask the children to think how they can make sure that they are not bullying when they want to exclude someone from joining in an activity.

Ask them to work in pairs and make a list of times when keeping someone out of a group is, in fact, bullying, for example, if they never let one certain person join, if they are unkind about keeping the person out, if they have no good reason for keeping them out, if they are discriminating against the person in some way. Share these reasons and make sure that everyone knows that this is bullying.

Ganging up

Ask the children to think of examples when two or more children gang up against one child in order to be unkind or keep the child out of the group. Have the children met this kind of bullying? If so, do they know what they should do?

Discuss this scenario

> There were only three Chinese boys in the class. Cheng, Huan and Gen were nearly always together and were good friends. When Cheng and Gen were away sick, Huan had no one to be with at break times. He wanted to join in some of the activities but the other children kept him out. They spoke unkindly about him having no mates and said he'd have to play on his own. No one in the class would be friendly to him and let him join in.

What could you do if you were in the class?

Ask the children if they could speak up against the other children and befriend Huan? How difficult would it be? How could they persuade their group of friends to let him join in?

Write a good ending

Ask the children to think of a good ending to this scenario. Think of a title that would show others that to keep excluding people is wrong and is bullying and that including them is the right thing to do.

7

Name-calling — younger children

Circle Time

Talk with the children about the names they like people to use when they are with them. Ask children to think whether the name that you use with them is their official first name or whether it is a shortened version. Ask volunteers who have a shortened first name to tell you what it is and what their official first name is.

Ask the children to draw a picture of themselves and to write their full first name together with any shortened version.

My first name is Manuel but people call me Manolo.

Nicknames

Come together to talk about their drawings and their names. Are any of these nicknames? Talk about nicknames and how some people like others to call them by a nickname because it can be really friendly. Explain that you should only use someone's nickname if they have given you permission; these may be family only names that the person is happy for their family to use but doesn't want anyone else to use. Ask the children if any of them has a nickname that they like people to use. Talk about these nicknames.

Name-calling

Explain that name-calling is very different from nicknames and that name-calling is a kind of bullying which excludes people from feeling part of a group or feeling happy with their friends. If you use someone's nickname without their permission they may also feel unhappy about it. The kinds of names that people use when they are name-calling are usually very horrid. These names often pick out and name something real but unkind about the child and are very hurtful. Talk with the children about what they should do if someone calls them names.

Tell a story

Jonty was six years old and not very good at his work in school. He needed help with his work and was often really upset when he couldn't do it. Sometimes he cried. Most of his friends tried to help Jonty but Sophie was really unkind and laughed when he got things wrong. In the playground one day she called him a 'stupid cry-baby'.

Ask the children to answer these questions:

How do you think Jonty felt when Sophie called him a stupid cry-baby?

What would you say to Sophie?

What would you say to Jonty?

What could you do or say to make Jonty feel better?

Ask the children to draw and write a good ending to this story.

Name-calling – older children

Discussion

Ask the children what they think of this old saying. Discuss what they say.

> 'Sticks and stones may break my bones but names will never hurt me!'

Has it happened to you?

Ask children if any of them have been called names and invite them to say how it made them feel. Write a list of these feelings words.

Read each of the feelings words and talk about each one.

Why do they do it?

Ask the children to think why people call others names.

Is it to make themselves feel big or important?

Is it to draw attention to themselves?

Is it so that people will think they are in control?

Can the children think of other reasons? Discuss all the reasons why they think people call others names and remind them that name-calling is bullying and causes people to feel excluded.

We felt:
horrid
out of things
hurt
unhappy
bad
unwanted
useless
shown up
embarrassed
in the limelight.

Good names

Discuss good names that you could use about other people. How would it make someone feel, for example, if people heard you say positive words about them, such as 'great', 'the best', 'a good mate'.

Look again at the list of 'feeling bad' words and ask children if they can suggest opposites for each one. Write the opposites against each one. Talk about the need to make people feel like this instead of making them feel like the words in the first list.

Write about it

Ask the children to write a story about someone who was called names. Ask them to:
- put themselves into the shoes of the person who was called names
- use some of the 'feeling bad' words when they write about what happened
- explain what someone said and did to make them feel better
- write a satisfactory outcome to the story.

A better saying

Ask the children to write a better saying than the one about name-calling not hurting. Read out some of these new and better sayings; choose one to display as a reminder.

7

Threatening behaviour – *younger children*

Circle Time

Talk to the children about promises and threats. Explain that promises are usually something good, something they will be pleased about. Threats, on the other hand, are usually something bad that they won't like.

Ask the children to tell you sentences using the word 'promise', for example, 'I promise I will help you with this.'

Ask the children to tell you sentences using the word 'threat' or 'threatens', for example, 'My dad threatens that he will not take me to the Zoo unless I am good.'

Threatening behaviour

Talk about grown-ups who may use threats to make sure we do the right thing. Talk about boys and girls who may use threats to make us do something that we know is wrong. Explain that often threats begin with, 'If you don't... then.' Ask the children to tell you what they should do if someone threatens to hurt them or to do something to them for some reason. Remind them that this is a kind of bullying and what they should do if someone at school threatens them.

I won't let you in

Talk about children who try to keep other children out of activities, games or groups. Sometimes these people threaten that they will harm them if they don't go away and sometimes they say they will let people in only if they do something wrong or give them something. Ask the children to raise a thumb if they have ever had this kind of thing happen to them. Remind them that they must always tell an adult if this kind of thing happens.

Finish the story

> Jo saw Tim and Mardig playing marbles outside Mardig's house on the pavement. Jo wanted to join in but Tim wouldn't let him unless he gave him his best marble. 'You mean I can't play?' said Jo. Tim said, 'I'll only let you join in if you give me that blue marble.' Mardig's big sister heard what Tim said and went outside at once...

Ask the children to suggest what Mardig's big sister might have said and done.

> What might Tim say and do?
>
> What might Jo say and do?

Ask the children to think about a good ending to the story and give their suggestions. Choose the best one and ask the children to draw and write about it.

Threatening behaviour – older children

Discussion

Discuss children feeling excluded because of another boy's or girl's threatening behaviour. Can they give examples of this, for example, not letting people play unless... or saying they want money or want them to give or do something before they let them join in? Make a note of the kinds of things they say and talk about the ethics of keeping people out by these kinds of threats.

How would they feel?

Talk about the feelings of someone who is excluded because of threatening behaviour. Ask the children to help you to make a list of these feelings. Discuss the effect on the schoolwork of someone who is excluded from joining in because of bullying. Explain that this would be a downward spiral because their work would suffer, teachers would become more demanding and the person left out would feel even more dispirited and their work would be even worse.

They would feel...

out of control, unaccepted, unwanted, lonely, friendless, dumb, unpopular, disliked, ignored.

What would you do?

Set the children a challenge; they are witnesses to some kind of threatening behaviour that is causing someone to be left out or ignored in class. Discuss the kinds of things that a witness can do. They will want to make sure that they themselves are not vulnerable. After discussion ask them to work in pairs to write about a friend of theirs being excluded because of threatening behaviour and to list the things they can do to help their friend.

Why would people threaten like this?

Talk about the characteristics of people who use threatening behaviour. What could cause them to behave like this? Can the children think of anything that adults, family or friends could do to make the threatening person want to stop this kind of behaviour?

Write a scenario

Ask the children to work in pairs to write a scenario where threatening behaviour by a bully could cause someone to feel excluded from class, school or sporting activities. Describe how the bully would feel and why he might want to behave like this. Describe how the bullied person would feel. Write a list of things that the bullied person could do to end the threatening behaviour. Write how the bully would feel once he could be made to realise the consequences of his actions.

Self-esteem — younger children

Circle Time

Talk to the children about self-esteem. Explain that self-esteem is how they feel about themselves, how confident they are in the classroom and how well they feel they are doing. A high self-esteem means they feel really good. A low self-esteem means they do not feel good about themselves.

Remind the children that they are all special and ask the children to think of the ways in which they feel good about themselves. Ask them to finish the sentence; 'I feel good about myself because...'

What makes you feel good?

Talk about the kinds of things that make us feel good about ourselves, for example, when we do good work, when someone praises us. Can you tell the children something that makes you yourself feel good? Ask them to finish the sentence: 'I feel good about myself when...'

I feel good about myself when I have finished reading a book.

Part of a group

Remind the children that we all need friends and feel good when we are part of a friendship group. Feeling that we belong makes us feel confident about ourselves and that gives us good self-esteem. People who belong to a group know that their friends in the group will support them and be on their side.

Supporting Other People Activity Sheet 1

Make sure the children know what 'supporting' means and talk about the things they can do to support people. Ask them to complete this activity sheet. Share their responses and talk about how it makes them feel when they support someone.

Responsibilities

Explain that we all have responsibilities as part of a group. Ask children to volunteer to tell the group any responsibilities that people have towards a group, for example, listening to others in the group, waiting their turn to speak, going along with the decision of the majority. Talk about giving and getting and ask the children to make two lists – what they give to a group and what they get from a group. Are some of the things the same?

Excluded from a group

Ask the children how they would feel if they were part of a group and then something happened to exclude them. How would they feel then? Would their self-esteem be high or low? What kinds of things could they do to get back into the group and begin to feel good about themselves again?

Self-esteem — older children

Talk to the children about the importance of good self-esteem. Explain that this means that they feel good about themselves and confident to join in groups and to work and play well. Ask the children to tell you the things that make them feel good about themselves. Some children may talk about having objects or things; try to steer them into thinking about personal qualities, abilities, staying power, skills, talents or gifts.

Feeling confident with good self-esteem

Explain that if you feel confident you will tackle new things with gusto, meet challenges, work things out. Explain that people who have good friendships and feel part of their group, feel fairly successful at work and play, have interests and spend leisure time profitably are usually confident people. People like this would be an asset to a group and would not usually be left out or excluded.

Ask the children to think of one person they know who has good self-esteem and to write a short paragraph of this person's qualities and why they are good to know.

Feeling hesitant, unsure, uncertain, shy

People with low self-esteem often find life difficult; will not be able to meet challenges, will have little to offer in the classroom or to friendship groups and may well be excluded because they are shy and quiet.

Raising self-esteem

Ask the children to think of what they can do to raise their own and other people's self-esteem.

Make a list of what they say and discuss each one.

Supporting Other People Activity Sheet 2

Ask the children to complete this activity sheet. Share their responses and talk about the feelings of both people who are supported and those who do the supporting.

Some suggestions for raising a child's self-esteem include encouraging the children to:

- think about what they are good at and give themselves praise for it

- be proud of their acheivements and skills

- talk to others they trust about how they are feeling

- talk about things which they might find difficult

- be good to themselves and treat themselves as special.

Can you do it?

Ask the children to look at the suggestions for raising self-esteem and to think about how they can raise their own. Ask each child to make a private list of what they can do to make themselves feel better about themselves. Ask them to think of someone they know who has low self-esteem and to think of what they can do or say to make this person feel good about himself. Remind them that excluding someone from a group or team can make the person's self-esteem plummet. We have no right to do this.

7

Supporting Other People Activity Sheet 1

My name is...

Draw a picture of you supporting a person in your class.

Write what you are doing to support this person.

I am...

Turn over the paper.

Draw a picture of someone in the class supporting you. Write what they are doing.

Supporting Other People Activity Sheet 2

My name is..

Draw the pictures; write at the side what you are doing to support them.

Draw you supporting a friend.	
Draw you supporting someone else.	
Draw you supporting a teacher.	

Turn over the paper.

Think about supporting someone at home.

Write what you are doing to support them and how it makes you feel when you support people.

Included or Excluded? Activity Sheet 1

My name is..

Draw pictures, write about it. Draw a ring around the correct sentence.

Draw a person helping you.	This person is...
	This is including.
	This is not including.
Draw a person praising you.	This person is...
	This is including.
	This is not including.
Draw a person not letting you play.	This person is...
	This is including.
	This is not including.

Turn over the paper. Draw a picture of you including someone. Write what you are doing.

Unit 7

Included or Excluded? Activity Sheet 2

My name is...

You can use this check list to elicit children's views on whether they think they have been excluded or not.

You could:

- go through the list, a few at a time, during Circle Times, inviting comments

- read it to young children, individually or in a small group and invite comments

- give it, or part of it, to older children to complete on their own.

	Did anyone, this week:	Tick here	Was it including?	Was it excluding?
1.	say you couldn't join in their game			
2.	ask you to play with them			
3.	say something like 'go away'			
4.	keep you out of a group			
5.	help you with your work			
6.	made a good joke with you			
7.	ask you to sit next to them			
8.	say they would help			
9.	make fun of you unkindly			
10.	play a good game with you			
11.	say you were their friend			
12.	make sure you were OK			
13.	say something good about you to someone else			
14.	share something with you			
15.	play outside with you			
16.	play well in a group with you			
17.	ask you to join their game			
18.	say they were glad they were a friend			
19.	praise you for good work			
20.	say you are special.			

Turn your paper over.

Draw two pictures; one of someone including someone and one where someone is keeping someone out.

Write about these pictures.

7

Think of a Story Activity Sheet 1

Think of a story you know well where someone was excluded, for example, Cinderella, Snow White, Hansel and Gretel or the Ugly Duckling. Draw a picture of the story.

Draw here.

Write here what you would have done to make sure the character wasn't excluded.

I would have...

Turn over and write a different ending.

Think of a Story Activity Sheet 2

Think of a story you know well where someone was excluded, for example, Cinderella, Snow White, Hansel and Gretel or the Ugly Duckling.

Write the main events of the story here.

Re-write the story with the main character being included and not excluded.

Turn over your paper.

Think about how you have changed the story. What has happened to it? Is it still a good story?

Write a critique of the new story and compare it with the original.

Extension activities for younger children

Research

Ask the children to work at home and ask people in their family if they have ever been bullied. Ask the children to write down any good advice that their family has for someone who is bullied. Discuss in school whether these pieces of good advice would work well.

Take home record sheet

Ask the children to make a record of one thing that they have learned during this unit that they didn't know before. Ask them to illustrate this record and to take it home to share with their family.

Investigation

Ask the children to ask their family about any nicknames that people used to call them. Ask them to talk about whether their family member was happy about people using this nickname; were they proud to have it or were they upset?

Poster

Ask the children to think of an anti-bullying slogan. Write these up on the board. Ask the children to choose one of the slogans and to make a multi-media poster using it.

Positive statements

Ask the children to help you to make a class list of positive statements to help prevent bullying and write these on the board.

Ask each child to choose one of these and to write it out on decorated card. Choose some to display around the room.

Making people feel good

Ask the children to help you to make a list of all the things that people can do to make other people feel good about themselves. Read through the list with the children and ask them to try to do at least one of these things each day.

Make another list of the things people can say to make other people feel good about themselves. Read through the list and ask the children to try to say at least one of these things to someone each day.

Extension activities for older children

Research

Ask the children to work in pairs and surf the internet for good anti-bullying advice. Ask each pair to write down what they think is the best advice on how to deal with bullying. Share this advice with the rest of the class. Ask them to choose the best advice to help someone who thinks they are being bullied, to write it on card and display it where everyone can see.

Take home record sheet

Write a list of all the parts in this unit on the board. Ask the children to use these as headings and to write a brief description of what they have learned from doing the work. Ask them to take their list home to share with their family.

Investigation

Tell the children that you want to find out what makes them feel good about themselves. Ask them to work in pairs and to write down two things that they or other people can say or do to make them feel good. Choose a spokesperson and ask each of these to read out their list to the class. Write these on the board, deleting any duplicates. Read through the list. Can anyone suggest other items to include? Ask the children to try to say or do at least one of these things every day.

Poster

Ask the children to work in groups to make a multi-media poster about raising someone's self-esteem. Ask them to choose a good title or slogan for their poster, for example, 'Help someone feel good today', or 'Make someone's day'.

Drama

Ask the children to work in pairs to do a silent role-play about making someone feel good. Tell them that they can use signs and body language but no words at all. Give them three minutes to discuss, then two minutes to do the role-play, change over for another two minutes. Come together as a group and talk about how this worked. Was the role-play successful? Did they make their partner feel good? Ask volunteers to show their role-play to the class.

7

Reflect and remember

This unit has been concerned with how behaviour such as bullying can make some children feel excluded and how children with low self-esteem rarely have the personal qualities to make sure they are not excluded. They have considered how to support others in order to make them feel good about themselves and to raise their self-esteem.

Circle Time

Ask the children to look at any displayed work and to think what they have learned from the activities and discussion in this unit and to finish the sentence:

'I have learned...'

Outside school

Remind the children that they have been looking at ways to improve their own self-esteem so that they will have the personal qualities to deal with bullying or with people who want to exclude them. Can they remember how to do this?

There are positive things they can do to raise self-esteem in their friends to make them feel good about themselves. Can they remember how to do this?

It could be you

Remind the children that they could be the ones doing the bullying, putting others down and making them feel small thus threatening or lowering self-esteem in others. They may do this because it makes them feel good or in control but they must remember that the kind of behaviour that makes someone else feel small or insignificant is not acceptable.

Activity sheets

You may want to display some of the activity sheets for everyone to read. Alternatively you may prefer the children to put them in their work folders.

Unit 8. Children with other special educational needs

Children in the classroom are often very resilient and accepting towards children with special needs. Many children take their classmates' behaviour and learning style for granted and see nothing wrong in any unusual actions, putting it down to the child's personality. Other children, however, may be inclined to be impatient with them or try to join in the behaviour.

We know that all children are special and that they may well all have special educational needs but in this unit we are concentrating on those children who may have learning difficulties, behavioural difficulties or personality conditions that don't make learning easy for them.

This unit seeks to help children to make sure that they don't, in any way, make children with special educational needs feel excluded from normal classroom activities under the following headings:

- Learning difficulties

- Behaviour difficulties

- Personality differences.

The paired activity sheets are mainly about different personalities.

'Helping Antonio' is pertinent to the unit on 'behaviour'.

'The Different Me's' activity sheets go with 'personality differences'.

The others could be used with any of the activities; you may need to explain to young children what an optimist and a pessimist is.

Useful websites

From the following website there are links to videos of autistic children talking about autism.

http://www.autism.org

http://www.healthnewsflash.com/conditions/tourette_syndrome.php

http://www.epilepsy.org.uk/info/behaviour.html

http://www.optimist.org/default.cfm?content=Vistors/visitors.htm

8

Learning difficulties – younger children

Circle Time

Talk to the children about the word 'clever'. Ask them to tell you what it means. Is everybody clever? Are some people cleverer than others? Are some people not clever at all? We are all clever at some things and not so clever at others. You can be clever at reading and not clever at drawing. You can be clever at clearing up and not clever at maths. Help them to understand that being clever at school work is not something we have any control over. Some people are and some people are not; it's just like having brown eyes, you are born that way. Some people think that being clever means you are just good at school work like sums or writing. We know that everyone is clever at some things. Remind the children that we are all special whether we are good at school work or not.

Doing our best

Explain that we can all do our best. Some people who are not clever can do better work because they try harder than children who are cleverer. Ask them to think of something they did recently that was their best; writing, reading, painting or sport. Ask them to finish this sentence: 'I was doing my best when I...'

I was doing my best when I played football even though I let a goal in.

Accept other's bests

Remind the children that we have to accept the best that people can do even if, to us, it doesn't look really good. If someone has tried hard, that's good. Remind them of a baby just learning to walk – they try their best and it takes a long time for them to master it; how we cheer when they do manage to walk.

We have a responsibility to accept what other children can do as their best, even if it doesn't seem really good to us.

Tell a story

> Sandy was seven years old and not very good at his work. He liked school because he had lots of friends and he was a good sport, always cheerful and helpful. Sometimes his teacher despaired of his work; it could be messy and badly written. The children in Class 3 were all very fond of Sandy and tried to help him to do better. One day a new boy Brett came to their school. Brett was very clever and did wonderful writing; he always got his maths right and the teacher was pleased with him. One day the teacher put up some of Sandy's work on the display board. It was a bit messy, but she knew that Sandy had tried his best. When Brett saw that it was next to his beautiful work he was not pleased. 'That's awful,' he said, 'that shouldn't be on the board, it's nowhere near good enough.' In the playground he mocked Sandy and wouldn't let him join in the game because he said he was no good.

What do you think the children in the class said to Brett? What do you think they said to Sandy? What would you have done if you had been there and Brett tried to exclude him? How would you have supported him?

Learning difficulties – older children

Discuss the similarities and differences between people. Ask them to tell you how we are all the same, for example, we have eyes, teeth. Ask them to tell you how we differ, for example, different coloured hair. Remind the children that these differences are mostly with us from birth and we have no control over them.

Talk about people who are very intelligent and those who have learning difficulties, reminding the children that these attributes too are genetic and we have no control over them. Someone who is intelligent is no better than someone with learning difficulties. Because we were born with different kinds of brains doesn't make one person superior to another.

Discuss: working to capacity

Ask the children to discuss as a class the following statement, without mentioning any children by name or group:

> 'If you're not clever you can't be expected to do good work.'

After the discussion, explain that some people who are not very clever do work very hard and produce good work by working longer and thinking harder than children who are clever but who don't work very hard.

Have the numbers of children who agreed with the above statement changed?

Discuss: not working to capacity

Ask the children to work in small groups or pairs and discuss the following statement:

> 'People who are intelligent always do the best work.'

Ask the groups to vote on whether they think the statement is true.

Redressing the balance

Ask the children to think how we can make sure that children who have learning difficulties can do the best for themselves. What help can we give them? Make a list of the suggestions. Read their lists. Have they included children supporting pupils with learning difficulties, setting lower, achievable targets, extra help from adults, making allowances? Does it include focussing on the strengths or special gifts that we all have, whether clever or not?

What can you do?

Ask the children to think about what they can do:

- if they themselves have learning difficulties
- if there are children with learning difficulties in their class.

Remind them that we all have a responsibility to include children in work and play and make sure that no one ever feels excluded.

Behaviour difficulties – younger children

Circle Time

Remind the children that we are all different in so many little ways. Talk to them about how we behave in different places and under different conditions. Ask them to think about places we go to and how we behave there then finish the sentence: 'When I am in the playground I...' Make a note of what the children say and continue the session with different places where we behave differently, for example, the classroom, on holiday, the football field, a swimming pool, in traffic.

We behave differently

Explain that we all have different personalities and ask the children to suggest ways in which we behave differently, for example, some people are quick to be angry, others are slow to move, some talk loudly and excitedly, others are quiet and listen more.

Ask the children to think of the kind of person they themselves are and to draw and write about two ways in which they behave.

Come together as a group and discuss what they have drawn. Help them to understand that we all have different behaviour patterns. Remind the children that we have a duty to behave sensibly and do the right things in the right places. We have to learn to control our feelings and not let them control us. We all have to respect other children and adults and think of their feelings.

I get really angry quickly when my brother messes with my toys.

I talk to the baby quietly so she feels good.

Children with behaviour difficulties

Remind the children that there are rules about how to behave and that some of these are not written down. Most children learn these rules at home and at school and know how to behave in different places. Explain that there are some children and grown-ups who have behaviour difficulties because of their personality or because of the way their brain works. These people have special needs and need a lot of help from everyone. It is not usually their fault if they behave in a different way from other people and we have to try to be patient and help them to learn new behaviour.

Helping Antonio Activity Sheet 1

Talk about Antonio, who has Autistic Spectrum Disorder (ASD). Explain that this is a medical condition and makes school difficult for him. Ask the children to complete this activity sheet and then talk about ways to help other children who behave like Antonio. If you have someone in your class or school who is named Antonio, choose a different name, such as Kolb or Tornig.

Write a story

Ask the children to write an illustrated story about a very young child with behaviour difficulties and to include in the story the kinds of things that would help him to learn how to behave in a more acceptable way. Share these stories.

Behaviour difficulties – older children

Discuss with the children how all people behave differently according to the place where they are. Ask them to supply examples of acceptable behaviour in various places. Discuss the importance of behaving appropriately wherever we are and of controlling our feelings and impulses; the necessity of thinking before we speak or act.

People with behaviour difficulties

Talk with the children about people, not necessarily children, who, through no fault of their own, find it difficult to behave appropriately. Can they tell you of any medical conditions which cause people to behave unsuitably? Remind the children that such people need our understanding and consideration, not condemnation, when they behave in this way.

What can you do?

Sometimes people find it hard or unpleasant to cope with those who have behaviour difficulties. Some laugh or mock people who behave in inappropriate ways. Remind the children that people with certain medical conditions who behave inappropriately do not realise that they are doing anything that is unacceptable or unusual. They need calm and understanding; they need help to manage their feelings. What they don't need are people who will stir up the atmosphere to make the situation worse.

Ask the children to work in pairs to think of examples of how they could diffuse a situation where someone is behaving in a difficult way. Share these with the class and discuss if they are good ideas.

Share this scenario

Antonio has Autistic Spectrum Disorder (ASD). He often behaves in an unususal way. It's hard for him to communicate and he avoids eye contact. People who speak to him are never quite sure if he has heard and understood what they said. Sometimes Antonio acts immaturely and says inappropriate things. He often taps his pencil over and over again and this is distracting for everyone. He often makes strange sounds.

Explain to the children that Antonio looks as normal as you or me. Ask them to think of what he needs and the qualities that people who work with Antonio must have so that they can help him.

I am a person with feelings just like you. I know I sometimes get things wrong. I try to understand you. All I want is for you to understand that I can't help the things I do. I want your respect and kindness.

Helping Antonio Activity Sheet 2

Ask the children to complete this activity sheet by writing how they can help him. They could draw cartoon pictures of them doing this in each small square. Remind them to do the activity on the other side. Discuss what the children write about Antonio.

Personality differences – younger children

Remind the children again that we are special and all different in so many ways. Talk about various personalities and how people react to different things in different ways. Talk about people who are always smiling and cheerful. Do they know people like this in their family at home? Ask volunteers to finish the sentence: 'Someone I know who is always smiling and cheerful is...'

Talk about the opposite; people who are often unhappy, worried and sad. Ask the children to raise a thumb if they know someone who is like this. What could they say to someone who is like this to make them feel less worried? Ask them to finish the sentence: 'I would say...'

What kind of person are you?

Ask the children to think about their own personality; are they always cheerful and friendly, are they sometimes cheerful and friendly or are they never cheerful and friendly? Do they look on the bright side or are they often gloomy and miserable?

The Different Me's Activity Sheet 1

Ask the children to think of the times when they are feeling different, happy, sad or neither. Ask them to complete this activity sheet. Share these pictures in Circle Time.

This is me. I smile a lot but sometimes I feel unhappy.

People are different

Remind the children that your personality is part of who you are and that children often have the kind of personality of their parents. There are things they can do to change the way they look at life. Can the children suggest things that a sad, unhappy child could do to make things better for himself?

What can you do?

Talk about how we can help people who are often sad and unsmiling. What kinds of things can we say and do to make them feel better? Collect the children's responses and make a list. This might make a good wall chart for you all to read occasionally.

Half Full or Half Empty? Activity Sheet 1

You may like to ask the children to complete this activity sheet now.

Include everyone

Remind the children that we have a responsibility to include all children even if their personality is very different from ours. It's not fair to exclude someone because they get angry quickly or because they are always moaning about things being unfair. We can make other people feel good about themselves if we think of their feelings and try to help them.

Personality differences – older children

Remind the children that one's personality may be inherited but that we are all in charge of the way we behave and can usually do something to make ourselves feel better if we really want to change.

Depressed people

Talk about the fact that some people are often depressed about themselves, their life and their abilities. We say that some people have a 'chip on their shoulder' and mean that they think that life is against them, they have low self-esteem and are rarely happy people to be around. It would be easy to exclude people who are like this. Can the children tell you some of the things they could do to help such people to make them feel good about themselves and feel that they have something to contribute. Make a list of these suggestions and discuss each one.

Put yourself in their shoes

Ask the children to think how it must feel to be depressed. Can they imagine how a depressed person's life must be? Ask them to think of examples of how a depressed person might behave; they may have seen people such as these on TV or read about them in the newspapers.

Half full, half empty

Talk about a glass partly filled with water and how some people see it as half full and others see it as half empty. These are optimists and pessimists. Ask them to think about what kind of person they themselves are and whether people like to be with them because they are fun and bubbly or whether they don't have many friends because they are often miserable and sad.

Half Full or Half Empty? Activity Sheet 2

Ask the children to complete this activity sheet. Discuss what they write.

Not their fault

Explain that some people who are very depressed are really ill and need a lot of help in order to start to live a happier life. This is a vicious circle; the person is depressed and so people don't want to be with them; this makes them more depressed and so on. If we exclude people like this from our friendship group we will make life worse for them. If we make sure we include such people and try to make life better for them we have a chance to help them to come out from this vicious circle.

8

Helping Antonio Activity Sheet 1

My name is..

This is Antonio's story.
Can you draw the pictures?

Antonio has autism.	Antonio doesn't look at people.	Antonio taps his pencil.
Antonio shouts a lot.	Antonio has no friends.	Antonio wants you to like him.

What could you do to help Antonio?
I could...

Turn over the paper and draw you helping Antonio to feel good about himself. What are you doing in your picture?

Helping Antonio Activity Sheet 2

My name is ....

Antonio has autism and finds school difficult.
Draw your picture of him and write how people in school can help him.

Antonio makes sudden noises.

He taps his pencil.

He can't look at you in the eye.

Antonio is in our class.

This is how we can help him.

We help Antonio by:	
We help Antonio by:	
We help Antonio by:	
We help Antonio by:	

Turn over the paper.
Write about how Antonio feels, alone in his own world.
Write about how he feels when people try to support him.

Unit 8

8

The Different Me's Activity Sheet 1

My name is ....

When I'm happy... 😊	
I look like this.	This is how I feel. I *feel*... This is what I do.

When I'm not happy ☹	
I look like this.	This is how I feel. I *feel*... This is what I do.

Turn over the paper.

Draw a picture of you a bit sad and trying to make yourself feel happy. What are you doing to try to make yourself feel happy?

Unit 8

The Different Me's Activity Sheet 2

My name is..

Draw yourself being happy and write how you feel and what you do and say. Write underneath how you behave.

Me being happy.	I feel...
	I do and say...
	I behave...

Draw yourself being unhappy and write how you feel and what you do and say. Write underneath how you behave.

Me being unhappy.	I feel...
	I do and say...
	I behave...

Turn over the paper.

Write about how you feel when you are behaving really well.

Write about how you feel when you know you are behaving badly.

Write what you can do to try to always behave well.

Optimist or Pessimist? Activity Sheet 1

My name is...

Draw yourself and write how you feel. Draw a ring around the sentence that tells whether you are an optimist or a pessimist.

Going to the swimming pool.	I feel...
	I am an optimist. I am a pessimist.
Going to a new restaurant.	I feel...
	I am an optimist. I am a pessimist.

Turn over the paper. Draw yourself being an optimist. What are you doing?
Write about your picture.

Optimist or Pessimist? Activity Sheet 2

This is Jill. She is worried about going on a school trip.

She is sure that things will go wrong and is really anxious about it.

Draw yourself and write what you would say to Jill.

I would say...

Here is Tatum. He is a bit too bold and adventurous, never worries and doesn't really take care.

He is going on the trip too. He knows that all will be well and that he will have a great time.

Draw yourself giving Tatum some good advice.

I would say...

Turn over and draw yourself. Write about the kind of person you are.

Half Full or Half Empty? Activity Sheet 1

My name is ....

Draw a glass with delicious juice half way up.

This is a glass with
delicious juice in it.

Do you think the glass is half full or half empty?

I think this glass is...

Draw a glass with nasty medicine half way up in it.

This is a glass with
nasty medicine in it.

Do you think the glass is half full or half empty?

I think this glass is...

Turn over the page and draw yourself with a glass of your favourite drink. Write how you feel when the glass is full. Write how you feel when the glass is empty.

Unit 8

Half Full or Half Empty? Activity Sheet 2

My name is...

Some people will see this glass half full and will be happy about that.
Draw a picture of someone who feels like this.

Some people will see this glass half empty and will be unhappy about that.
Draw a picture of someone who feels like this.

Write about each of these people.

The half empty glass person...

The half full glass person...

Turn over the page and write about you – are you a half full glass person or a half empty glass person?

Extension activities for younger children

Research

Ask the children to talk to their families at home about optimists and pessimists. Ask them to ask all members of their family whether they are an optimist or a pessimist. Ask the children to make a list with each person's name and to write alongside whether they are an optimist or a pessimist. In school count up the total numbers of people who say they are optimists and pessimists. Are there more optimists or pessimists?

The optimist creed Investigation

http://www.optimist.org/default.cfm?content=Vistors/visitors.htm

Visit this website to see the optimist creed. There is a copy of it on the page after next. Read through and talk about each one with the children. Ask them to think of one point that they would like to put in a class optimist creed.

Put yourself in their shoes

Ask each child to draw a large outline of a shoe on a piece of A4 paper.

Ask them to think of a happy person they love and to write this person's name outside the shoe. Ask them to draw this person inside the shoe outline doing some of the good and loving things that they do. Ask them to write outside the shoe:

'This is................................. I would like to be in their shoes.'

Poster

Ask children to design an optimist poster. It must have some kind of slogan or statement, be colourful and attractive. Talk about each poster and ask the children to vote on one to display in the classroom.

Drama

Ask the children to work in pairs with one of each pair playing the part of someone who is unhappy or sad. The other person has to try to cheer them up. Give the children three minutes to talk about what they will say or do. Allow only three minutes for the role-play and then ask the children to change over. Come together as a class to talk about how they felt when they were playing these parts. Was it easy or difficult to cheer the person up? What kinds of things did they do to cheer them up?

Investigation

Ask the children to find out more about people with special needs and behaviour difficulties. Write the name of each difficulty on the board and talk about each one. Help the children to understand that people with behaviour difficulties need help and understanding.

Take home record sheet

Ask the children to make a record of one thing that they have learned during this unit that they didn't know before. Ask them to illustrate this record and to take it home to share with their family.

Extension activities for older children

Research

Ask the children to find out more about conditions that make children behave differently, for example, Tourette syndrome, Autism and Asperger Syndrome. Can they find out how these conditions were named, what the symptoms are and how these can be treated? Remind them that websites are a rich source of information.

Investigation

Find out exactly what an optimist is by looking at this website:

http://www.optimist.org/default.cfm?content=Vistors/visitors.htm

A class optimist creed

Ask the children if they can write an optimist creed especially for your class. There is an example of an optimist creed on the next page.

Poster competition

Ask the children to design a poster which exhorts people to be cheerful, positive and look on the bright side. It should have a slogan or message.

Arrange the posters and ask the children to vote on the one most likely to convey this message. Display this one.

Drama

Select various scenarios and ask the children to work in small groups to present them, first as optimists and then as pessimists.

The children may have their own ideas for scenarios or you could use the following:

Meeting someone for the first time who is popular and great fun.

Going to a new class.

Meeting a new teacher for their class for the first time.

Handing in a piece of work.

Going on a school outing.

Take home record sheet

Write a list of all the parts in this unit on the board. Ask the children to use these as headings and to write a brief description of what they have learned from doing the work. Ask them to take their list home to share with their family.

8

The Optimist Creed

Promise yourself-

To be so strong that nothing can disturb your peace of mind.

To talk health, happiness and prosperity to every person you meet.

To make all your friends feel that there is something in them.

To look at the sunny side of everything and make your optimism come true.

To think only of the best, to work only for the best, and to expect only the best.

To be just as enthusiastic about the success of others as you are about your own.

To forget the mistakes of the past and press on to the greater achievements of the future.

To wear a cheerful countenance at all times and give every living creature you meet a smile.

To give so much time to the improvement of yourself that you have no time to criticize others.

To be too large for worry, too noble for anger, too strong for fear, and too happy to permit the presence of trouble.

http://www.optimist.org/default.cfm?content=Vistors/visitors.htm

Reproduced here with kind permission of:

Dana L. Thomas

Executive Assistant

Optimist International

4494 Lindell Blvd.

St. Louis MO 63108 USA

who says that, 'The Optimist Creed is public domain – you may use it freely.'

Reflect and remember

This unit has been concerned with children who are different in some way and who will need respect and help from the other children in the class.

Circle Time

Ask the children to look at any displayed work and to think what they have learned from the activities and discussion in this unit and to finish the sentence:

'I have learned...'

It could be you

Remind the children that all children have special needs; it's just that some children need a little more help with work at school. Remind them that they have a part to play in helping to raise self-esteem in other children and that it is important never to make less able children feel insecure or unhappy.

Various personalities

Remind the children that we are all different and that we can all feel different on different days and in different circumstances. We all have days when we find it difficult to behave well, especially if we feel that things are not going our way.

Optimists

Ask the children to look again at your positive statements and optimist work around the classroom. Remind them that it is not always easy to see the bright side of things and behave well but that it gets easier with practice.

Outside school

Help the children to remember that looking on the bright side and being positive and optimistic is not reserved for school. They will find that life is rosier and things go better for them if they can try to be a cheerful and happy person.

The world and you

Read this saying:

> Laugh and the world laughs with you;
>
> Weep and you weep alone.

Talk with the children about what this saying really means.

Can they write a new saying with the same meaning?

8

Appendix

Resources: Books, websites and posters

Bliss, T. & Tetley, J. (2007) Circle Time. A Resource Book for Primary and Secondary Schools.
A Lucky Duck Book. Paul Chapman Publishing, Sage Publications, London.

Bornman, J., Collins, M. & Maines, B. (2004) Just the Same on the Inside – understanding diversity and supporting inclusion in Circle Time.
A Lucky Duck Book. Paul Chapman Publishing, Sage Publications, London.

Collins, M. (2004) But is it Bullying?
A Lucky Duck Book. Paul Chapman Publishing, Sage Publications, London.

Collins, M. (2007) Circle Time for the Very Young, 2nd edition.
A Lucky Duck Book. Paul Chapman Publishing, Sage Publications, London.

DfEE (2001) Promoting Children's Mental Health within Early Years and School Settings.

Drifte, C. (2001) Special Needs in Early Years Setting.
David Fulton Publishers, Taylor Francis, London.

MacConville, R. (2007) Looking At Inclusion. Listening to the voices of young people.
A Lucky Duck Book. Paul Chapman Publishing, Sage Publications, London

O'Hanlon, J. & Wootten, A. (2007) Using Drama to Teach Personal, Social and Emotional Skills.
A Lucky Duck Book. Paul Chapman Publishing, Sage Publications, London.

Rae, T. (2007) Dealing With Feeling. A Resource Pack.
A Lucky Duck Book. Paul Chapman Publishing, Sage Publications, London.

RNIB E & E (2001) Including Children with Impaired Vision in Early Years Settings.
This booklet describes how a child with sight problems can take a full part in play and learning alongside children who are fully sighted.

RNIB, Mobility and Independence, assessment and evaluation scheme, early skills. Promoting equality. Free publication. Email helpline@rnib.org.uk

This ringback book helps teachers to assess abilities and needs of the partially sighted. It has a comprehensive bibliography.

Roffey, S. (2006) Circle Time for Emotional Literacy.

Paul Chapman, Sage Publications, London.

Weatherhead, Y. (2008) Creative Circle Time for Early Years. A Resource Pack.

A Lucky Duck Book. Paul Chapman Publishing, Sage Publications. London.

White, M. (1998) Magic Circles. Building Self-esteem through Circle Time.

A Lucky Duck Book. Paul Chapman Publishing, Sage Publications, London.

Useful websites

Visit Teachernet online to download or order 'Implementing the Disability Discrimination Act in Schools and Early Years Settings'.

http://www.uni.edu/coe/inclusion/philosophy/philosophy.html

http://www.standards.dfes.gov.uk/primary/wholeschool/inclusion/e/inclusion/

http://www.dwp.gov.uk/aboutus/provisions-dda.pdf

http://www.teachernet.gov.uk/wholeschool/sen/disabilityandthedda/

http://www.enableme.org.uk/

http://www.britishsignlanguage.com/

http://www.bbc.co.uk/health/conditions/

http://lenmac.tripod.com/celebrities.html

http://www.wheelpower.org.uk/

http://www.paralympics.org.uk/

http://www.reddisability.org.uk/index-text-only/DisSport.htm

http://www.omsakthi.org/religions.html

http://www.krysstal.com/borrow.html.

http://www.omsakthi.org/religions.html

http://www.krysstal.com/borrow.html.

http://www.oraldeafed.org/movies/index.html

http://www.stammertrust.co.uk/pdf/drawings.pdf

http://www.collectbritain.co.uk/collections/dialects/

http://en.wikipedia.org/wiki/List_of_languages_by_first_written_accounts#Before_1000_BC

http://en.wikipedia.org/wiki/Language#Formal_languages

http://surnames.behindthename.com/

http://www.oraldeafed.org/movies/index.html

http://www.cockneyrhymingslang.co.uk/slang/apples_and_pears

http://www.stammertrust.co.uk/pdf/drawings.pdf

http://www.collectbritain.co.uk/collections/dialects/

http://www.vistawide.com/languages/language_statistics.htm

http://oncampus.richmond.edu/academics/education/projects/webunits/greecerome/Greeceroles1.html

http://www.stratfordhall.org/ed-boysgirls.html

http://findarticles.com/p/articles/mi_m2294/is_9-10_53/ai_n16084036

http://www.media-awareness.ca/english/resources/tip_sheets/gender_tip.cfm

http://findarticles.com/p/articles/mi_m2294/is_9-10_53/ai_n16084036

http://www.autism.org

http://www.healthnewsflash.com/conditions/tourette_syndrome.php

http://www.epilepsy.org.uk/info/behaviour.html

http://www.optimist.org/default.cfm?content=Vistors/visitors.htm

Privileged People

We all like to be privileged at times, but not all the time.

Unit 1

In a wheelchair you can do exciting things.

Unit 2

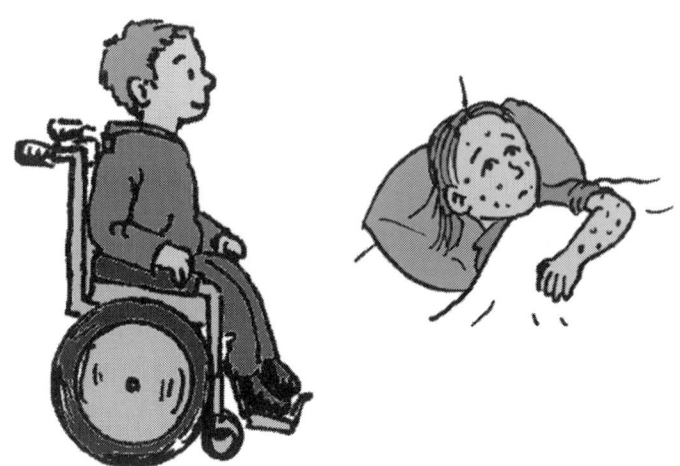

How we are all the same
and different.

Unit 3

Let's include everybody in our games.

Unit 4

We may all look different but we're all the same inside.

Unit 5

We may speak differently but everyone should be able to join in.

Unit 6

Who says it's a girl's job?
Anyone can do anything no
matter what their gender!

Unit 7

We know how to act towards each other, not to bully and to think of people's feelings and to raise their self-esteem.

Unit 8

We are all special. Let's make
sure we include everybody.